THE TWELVE COMMANDMENTS FOR SMALL BUSINESS™

I. Thou shalt be well organized

II. Thou shalt plan thy work and work thy plan

III. Thou shalt conserve cash

IV. Thou shalt sell effectively

V. Thou shalt negotiate well

VI. Thou shalt serve thy employees

VII. Thou shalt obey the law

VIII. Thou shalt keep excellent records

IX. Thou shalt be tax wise

X. Thou shalt be high tech

XI. Thou shalt be properly insured

XII. Thou shalt balance thy life

XIII. Thou shalt deliver fine quality

THE

XII

COMMANDMENTS
FOR
SMALL BUSINESS

THE

XII

COMMANDMENTS
FOR
SMALL BUSINESS

*A Practical Guide
to Beating the Odds*

RICHARD J. SACKS

Jefalt Press Co.
St. Charles, Missouri

Published by Jefalt Press
213 Main Street
St. Charles, MO 63367

Publisher's Cataloging-in-Publication Data
Sacks, Richard J.

The twelve commandments for small business / Richard J. Sacks. –
St. Charles, MO : Jefalt Press Co., 2007.

p. ; cm.
ISBN: 0-9779307-0-X
ISBN 13: 978-0-9779307-0-8

1. Small business. 2. Success in business. I. Title.

HD2341 .S23 2006
338.6/42—dc22   2006925597

Project coordination by Jenkins Group, Inc • www.BookPublishing.com
Interior design by 1106 Design
Cover design by Chris Rhoads

Printed in the United States of America
11 10 09 08 07 • 5 4 3 2 1

To B.

CONTENTS

ACKNOWLEDGMENTS

The information and insights in this book result from my being fortunate enough to have been exposed to many fascinating people over the years. I have worked with both the honorable and dishonorable among us. I thank each of them for making a contribution to my frame of reference.

I will not name any of the dishonorable, but I do want to name some of the honorable:

As corny as it sounds, I will start with my fifth- and sixth-grade teacher, Florence Polakoff, who showed me the value of cultural diversity. Next, is one of my student advisers at CCNY, Laura Farrar, who exposed me to the concept of intellectual problem solving. Joel Sollender, my boss at my first big job out of college, who taught me the importance of investing my personal values in my job. And James VanCleave, the only person I ever worked for who always was one step ahead of me. Each of these people made a profound contribution to my life. I'm quite certain that none of them is aware of that fact.

I also want to thank all of the people who helped me to create this book. Dick Welsch, Ron O'Connor, Lee Rohlf and Lazslo Domjan played pivotal roles. The people who were kind enough to review the manuscript and offer their invaluable feedback, for which I am grateful, include: Rudy Beck, Greg Bedell, Joyce Follman, Paul Lambi, Jane McNeil, Ed Morris, Doug O'Connor, Greg Prestemon, Jack Rickner, Maria Taxman and Tim Willard.

And finally, to my family and near family. My wife Bev, and my children Jeff, Ally and Teala, who have lived this crazy life along with me, and without whom I could not have accomplished so much. And to Trish Binek, my "day wife" (with whom Bev conspired) who assisted me with her many talents for almost a decade and a half.

INTRODUCTION

No small business ever failed because the owner ran out of money. Small businesses fail because the owners run out of time.

Using trial and error to find your way to success in business can take a long time. All the while, the meter keeps running, counting off dollars minute-by-minute and second-by-second until the costs exhaust your limited supply of capital. And then it's over. You can't afford to pay for more time to complete your learning curve.

Most people know the old joke about the young musician standing on a Manhattan street corner. The student asks a stranger: "How do I get to Carnegie Hall?" The stranger replies: "Practice, practice, practice."

Funny thing. We're expected to practice and prepare for most major things we do in life—but not for starting a business. Broadway actors spend months in rehearsal before they're allowed to open. NASCAR drivers are told to take practice runs around the track before the race. Professional golfers play practice rounds before the tournament. All of these people have trained their entire careers. But they still need practice.

Small-business owners? They're expected to open for business without experience and knowing practically nothing about what they're doing. Yet they get no opportunity to practice before the curtain rises. You wouldn't expect to go to boot camp and use live ammunition the very first day—but you're expected to do essentially the same thing when you open a business. It's no wonder so many businesses get "killed."

The death toll of small businesses runs into the hundreds of thousands each year. Yet eternally optimistic entrepreneurs keep coming, ignoring the odds, trying to achieve business success.

The only way to do something about small-business failure and to stop the wholesale killing of small businesses is to do like every successful professional: rehearse, train, practice. That's what *The Twelve Commandments for Small Business* is all about.

This book is a dry run through the maze of business. It takes you through the many obstacles, rules and opportunities business owners face as soon as they open their doors. This is your script, your checklist, your playbook to be an entrepreneur.

Whether the issue is setting up and organizing your business, hiring and managing people, or making sure you stay on the right side of the law, *The Twelve Commandments* will provide you with the briefing you need to run out onto the playing field. If you're already in business, it will give you a chance to catch up on some things you're still consuming capital to learn.

We know that small businesses fail because they run out of the time it takes to figure things out. *The Twelve Commandments for Small Business* will save you time, and therefore money, by helping you complete your learning curve more quickly. Hopefully, you'll even have some capital left.

The more you know about the track you will be running on, the more likely you are to finish at the head of the pack. Remember, it all boils down to practice, practice, practice.

Commandment 1:
Thou Shalt Be Well Organized

**Develop your own system to organize
every aspect of your business.
The difference between being busy and
being productive is in the level of your
organization skills.**

Think of the world of business as a speed-ing bullet train. You'd like to board the train and become a successful member of the business community. The good news is that anyone can board. The bad news is that many people often stand at a dead stop while the train passes them by. You need to get up to speed and step aboard. But first, you need a ticket to ride.

You will be required to identify yourself and explain why you want to board. You will have to decide how you will pay for your place onboard and where you will fit into the whole scheme of things. Where will you plug in?

Forming an organization that fits into the existing rules and structures is your first task.

"Thou shalt be well organized," then, can be none other than the first of *The Twelve Commandments for Small Business*. It's the bedrock commandment on which all the others are built.

The world of business, at first glance, appears to be somewhat chaotic. To survive and prosper, however, you must avoid chaos at all cost. Unfortunately, chaos is like a contagious disease and your business is particularly susceptible. If we observed the final days of failed small businesses, most often we'd see chaos.

You can avert chaos by organizing well and getting your arms around your basic structure. You establish a firm foundation upon which to stand and maintain a clear identity. When a crisis hits, knowing what resources you have and who is responsible for what is the quickest way to resolve it. If you have no clue, you will develop a survival mentality of "every man for himself" and give way to chaos.

With too many tasks, too few hands and too little experience, you have a hard enough time maintaining order when things are calm. Try it when you're desperate for success.

Helping you to successfully maneuver even when things are about to unravel is the heart and soul of this commandment.

ORGANIZING CORRECTLY

In selecting a form of organization, you face two considerations: How you will fit into the legal system and how you will fit into the tax system.

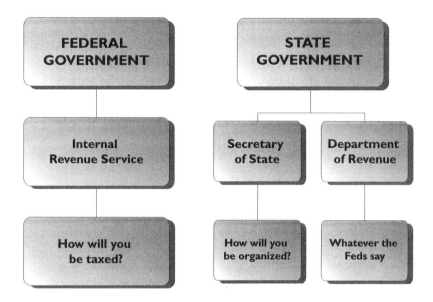

When choosing your *legal* form of organization, you will be dealing with your state government, specifically, your secretary of state. When choosing your form of organization for *tax* purposes, you will be dealing with the federal government, specifically, the Internal Revenue Service. Fortunately, the feds will accept whatever form you tell your state and your state will accept whatever tax arrangements you make with the feds.

Legal organizations come in four flavors. You choose one from the following:

- Sole proprietorship
- Partnership
- Corporation
- Limited liability company, known as LLC

An important function of your state's secretary of state is to help commerce succeed within the state. To do this, the secretary keeps track of who is doing business within state borders by requiring annual reports to be filed. One reason businesses must register is so people can find out who owns a company in case legal issues arise. And this is the crux of your organizational decision: To the world at large, the form of a company's organization is a liability issue. Is the company a corporation that, in the eyes of the law, is a legal individual separate from you? Is the company a sole proprietorship or a partnership that, in the eyes of the law, is indistinguishable from you personally? Whose name is on the contract, and whose assets, and what assets are at risk?

A **sole proprietorship** is the most basic form of business organization. Hang a shingle, open the doors and you're in business. The company need not register with the state. Essentially, your company and you are inseparable. Because in a sole proprietorship you *are* the company, nothing separates you legally as an individual from the company itself. In the eyes of the law, the company's business is seen as an extension of your personal affairs. The ramifications are huge. If a customer is injured in your shop and sues for damages, he or she can go after your business assets and your personal assets—your house, for example—to satisfy the claim should the person win the suit.

A **partnership** is nothing more than a sole proprietorship with multiple owners. As such, it offers no legal separation between company and owners.

A **corporation** is a legal entity with a life of its own and even has a tax identification number similar to your Social Security number. A corporation can sign contracts in its name, be sued and survive its owners. Best of all, even if you own 100 percent of a corporation's stock, as most small-business owners do, you are still just a shareholder and nothing more.

As such, you are usually not personally liable for the corporation's obligations. So, if the corporation is sued, only corporate assets are at risk, not the personal assets of its shareholders. This separation between the corporation and its owners is called the "corporate veil" and is a bit of personal protection worth its proverbial weight in gold. A word to the wise, though: The corporate veil can be "pierced" under certain circumstances. (That's why it's not called an "iron curtain.") Your attorney can explain this issue in detail.

A **limited liability company (LLC)** is the newest player on the block. It is the form of organization most recommended for small businesses. An LLC is a hybrid form of organization which was established to provide the legal protections of the corporate veil without having to go through some of the complexities of incorporating. Basically, the LLC is a sole proprietorship or partnership with limited liability. It is very attractive and simple to establish.

Once you have told the state which form of organization you prefer, you're ready to let the feds know how you want to be taxed. I didn't say "if" you wanted to be taxed, I said "how."

A company has two ways to pay its taxes: It can pay the taxes itself, or you can pay the taxes for it. If you selected sole proprietorship or partnership, you always pay the taxes directly on your personal tax return every April 15. No choice. If you selected corporation or LLC, you can choose.

The way you inform the feds of how you want your taxes to work is known as an "election." If you chose corporation, you can decide to pay the taxes with your personal return by electing to be an S-Corporation. An S-Corporation is known as a "pass-through" entity because the income of the corporation "passes through" to the personal returns of the shareholders.

If you do not elect to be an S-Corporation, you will automatically be a C-Corporation, which pays its own taxes every March 15.

Whichever you choose, a C or an S, the decision is not necessarily set in stone. You can change from an S to a C or a C to an S, with very strict limitations. Only your tax adviser can handle these issues.

Today's hot ticket corporate structure is the LLC. An LLC has members as opposed to shareholders, and allows the owners to select whichever method of taxation they prefer— as either a pass-through entity or a non-pass-through entity.

Selecting an organization and tax format for your company is like choosing a major in college. You are required to make a decision that can have an impact on the rest of your life, but without the experience to know what is really right for you. It's a mistake to make these decisions without guidance. Make sure you get some.

PLANNING YOUR INTERNAL STRUCTURE

A client of mine, an ex-senior VP at a good-sized firm, retired and followed his dream, opening a little business of his own. He told me his awakening to what it meant to be a small-business owner came the day he discovered that postage meters do not fill themselves with postage. He never thought about it before. He never had to. Apparently, someone else just … well … did it. Thinking back, he's not even sure who that someone was. Now it was up to him.

That's small business in a nutshell. In your company, if you don't do it (pick any task) or assign someone to do it, it won't get done. It's all up to you. So better learn to deal with it.

An excellent way to keep track of who is supposed to be filling the postage meter is to create a "functional organization chart." Contrary to popular belief, an organization chart is not just a visual representation of who reports to whom and who has the power in the company. It does that, certainly, but only secondarily. Primarily, an organization chart should be functional—a visual representation of who is responsible for what tasks in the company.

Essentially, every business, large or small, has the same basic organizational structure. From Microsoft to microbreweries to tiny mom and pop stores, one chart fits all. The only difference is the depth of the chart.

Every Company's Organization Chart

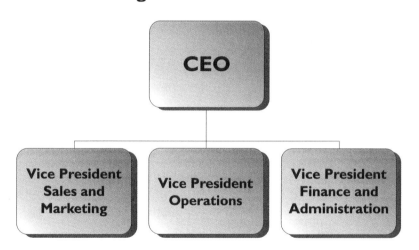

The CEO sits in the top box, umbilically connected to the VP of sales and marketing, the VP of operations and the VP of finance and administration. All the tasks required to make the company go are filtered through those three departments. The CEO, preeminently perched, has ultimate responsibility for everything in the company. It's the price you pay for being top dog. All the others, from the most senior VP to the newest hire in the mailroom, are simply support staff, doing their bits to make it all work.

Your Organization Chart

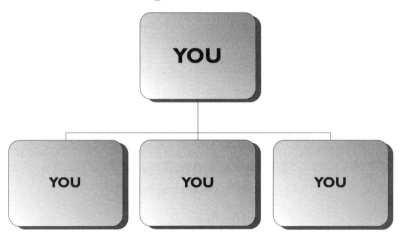

Now, about your company's organization chart: The good news is … you're top dog! The bad news is … you're the *only* dog. An intimidating, even harsh reality. Let's ignore the fear factor for the moment. What's important is to understand what the chart's telling you. The message is basic and critical: It's up to you to recharge the postage meter. If you don't do it, or assign someone to do it, it won't get done. Though it's not written down anywhere that you have to do everything yourself, it is written down that everything has to be done. The first challenge, then, is to figure out the myriad things that need to be done.

Each of the main departments in your company—sales and marketing, operations, and finance and administration—is responsible for a specific grouping of tasks. Learning what the tasks are for each department will give you a listing of everything that needs to be done—from advertising to order-taking, from making product to shipping it, from billing customers to collecting their money. Create those lists and you'll have an organized, compartmentalized overview of what needs to be done to make your business go. Then you can begin to consider how to make it all happen—in an orderly, organized fashion. Seen in that light, an organization chart is not the height of overkill most business owners believe. Rather, it's an indispensable weapon in the fight against chaos—and a dynamic management tool to boot.

A properly used organization chart will help you understand your business. It won't eliminate a crisis, but it will help to define it. In the unsettled atmosphere of most small businesses, when something's wrong, it's nearly impossible to separate symptoms from diseases. You can wind up responding to effects and not causes. An organization chart, with its careful outline of tasks, makes it easier to pinpoint root problems and, thus, appropriate solutions.

The chart will also help you understand where you need help. For openers, practically every box on the chart will have your name in it. Your goal is to get out of most of the boxes. By understanding the functions within your own company, it will quickly become apparent which box you want to vacate first. When things are constantly unwinding and crisis management is a way of life, you will soon realize you need help—but with which tasks? The chart will tell you because it will underscore the key tasks that you are consistently not doing.

When you bring employees on board, the chart will help define their jobs. Though a small business needs a "pitch-in" mentality throughout, employees also need to know their bottom-line responsibilities. Not knowing where you stand is a phenomenal stress producer. Employees like to know how they fit in. The organization chart will provide employees with the answers they seek and allow your managers to manage effectively, too.

Finally, the organization chart, with its status-conferring hierarchical structure, can be an excellent means of rewarding and retaining employees. Titles can be a very inexpensive fringe benefit.

PLANNING GROWTH

When a contingent of Japanese car makers was asked their thoughts after touring a gargantuan U.S. automobile plant, their response was telling: "We would never build one so big." To us, the plant was a wonder under one roof. To the Japanese, it was too big to manage properly. Whose gut would you go with?

Bigger is not always better. For small-business people hustling for success that thought is incredibly counter-intuitive, if it's thought about at all. But it's true, nonetheless.

If your business doubled tomorrow, could the company handle it? Likely not. Emotionally, fast growth may be satisfying—until it swamps the business altogether. The chicken-producing companies that "won" the initial orders when fast food chains began serving chicken were invariably overwhelmed. Visions of fortune became a struggle for survival. What they "won" was simply too much, too fast. Growth, like anything else in your business, needs to be managed carefully.

Growth creates stress in a business. It's difficult and disruptive. Even though your company may be well situated and capable of handling those stresses, growth alone is not a reason for growing. If growth isn't having a positive impact on your bottom line, what's the point? Would you rather earn $200,000 owning a $2 million company, or make the same money owning a $10 million company? In the $10 million version, you've multiplied headaches—exponentially—while not necessarily earning a dime more. What have you really achieved? Size and nothing else.

If the growth is positioning the company for an appropriate and sought-after "next step," it may be wise. But guard against the urge to grow just to be growing. Growth for the sake of growth is the subtlest of killers. Huge companies fail because of over-expansion. Ever wonder how a company can lay off 10,000 employees on a single day?

Be wary, too, of illogical growth. That is, growth in a direction away from your core business. Act cautiously in adding a line of products unrelated to the products you're already producing. If your original plan doesn't seem to be working, the easiest thing for you to do is to try something else. After all, if you can't score a touchdown, why not try for a home run? That notion is nonsense. The one has absolutely nothing to do with the other. Changing games is not a wise option. Yet desperate businesses do it all the time.

Growth equals success only if the business can cope with it and if it takes you where you truly want to go. But where do you want to go?

Commandment II: Thou Shalt Plan Thy Work and Work Thy Plan

A well thought out business plan is the foundation for business direction and growth. Forget pie in the sky projections, be pragmatic and realistic. Always remember you have to work thy plan as well as plan thy work.

If you're into sports, you know the best coaches stick with their game plans even when the going gets rough. They realize their cool, clear-headed pre-game analysis, made in the quiet of their offices, with the counsel of their assistants, is a far more reliable guide to victory than heat-of-the-moment, sideline decisions will ever be. So it is with business.

A business plan is like a coach's game plan. You take the time to think through a master plan that puts together the effort and resources to accomplish a goal: to create and successfully operate a business. Incredibly, these best-laid plans are often filed and forgotten as soon as the shop doors open. It's as if planning for the business had been nothing more than an elaborate mental exercise. Soon critical decisions are being made without referring to the game plan.

"Winging it" is never a wise business strategy. If you let emotion trump intellect, you're headed for disaster. Basing decisions on emotion might satisfy you at the moment, but you're doing little more than gambling. You designed your business plan for a reason. Like a good coach, rely on it.

This chapter focuses on the second commandment, "Thou shalt plan thy work and work thy plan." In it, we'll explore business planning and how to make your plan a dynamic navigational tool. We'll look at risk, examine sources of capital and consider budgeting techniques. Finally, we'll examine exit strategies should worst come to worst.

The best coaches know the value of a game plan, and they're "merely" coaches. You, as a small-business owner, are both coach *and* lead player. A well-considered and smartly executed game plan is doubly critical for you.

FITTING INTO YOUR PLANS

Know thyself. When it comes to your business, you are the giver of life and the sustainer of life. That's what it means to be a small-business owner. Making yourself aware of how you fit into your own plans is your first and most important task. So, what's it all about? What are you trying to accomplish?

Exactly <u>what</u> are you trying to accomplish?

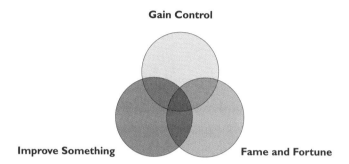

Do you know exactly why you decided to embark on this journey? Earning piles of money and a healthy dose of fame are perfectly acceptable motivating factors. Gaining control of your professional life is another valid goal. Tired of condemning yourself to obnoxious bosses and untimely downsizings? Or maybe you've got a better idea. Bravo! And best of luck. Whatever your reason for rolling the dice, what matters most is that *you* understand the grail you're seeking—and that you consider the sacrifices you'll be called upon to make.

I know you're not independently wealthy and able to plunk down dollars willy-nilly. If you were, you wouldn't be starting a business from scratch. You would more likely buy an existing, successful business. So, money will be tight. But on top of money, starting a business will demand significant sacrifices from every cell of your body—and family members' bodies too.

First, the money: Where will it come from? Savings? A second mortgage? Retirement plan? Each will significantly affect your life. Time, too, is coveted by a budding business—your time in particular. Nine-to-fives will be a thing of the past. Are you and your family ready, willing and able for what that means? Gone, too, will be the comfort and security of a steady payroll check and company benefits. Can you and the family deal with that? Whatever decisions are made, be upfront with everyone concerned. You'll need everyone's support.

Starting a business involves risk. Risk runs the continuum from no risk to calculated risk to foolish risk. Which are you prone to? There is no right or wrong answer. You are who you are, but if you are totally risk-averse, stop right now. Business is inherently risky. If the thought of signing a lease for office space makes your forehead damp and sleeping difficult, better to recognize it upfront. You will not have a happy time of it.

Foolish risk—playing double or nothing at the poker table—is a terrible business practice. If you thrive on that kind of risk, you better have resources to fall back on when you lose your business by taking ridiculous chances.

That leaves calculated risk. This is where you understand the variables and all the possible outcomes and are willing to live with however things work out. If this is who you are, proceed.

PLANNING TO MEET YOUR GOALS

For all its importance, your business plan is a simple document. It lists all you know about your business and all you hope for it. So, list what you know, find out what you don't, add some speculation, format it—and you're done! Follow the principle of KISS—keep it simple, stupid—and you'll do fine. Use "straightforward and simple, neither unique nor exotic" as your business-planning mantra, and that's how your business will evolve.

A small business is all about survival, not about reinventing the wheel.

Trying to be unique for openers is expensive and you can't afford it. So, study your competitors and copy them. They've been around for a while. They've figured out things you haven't even considered. Learn from them. That's not heresy. It's your best guide to success. Certainly, your business will have unique aspects, based on things you don't like about the competition. Those aspects will become your competitive edge.

Factor in what assets and resources you have and what you want to do. Then map out how you can make it happen within those boundaries. The business plan essentially recites the answers to each of the following:

- What does the business do?
- For whom does it do it?
- How does it do it?
- Who makes it happen?
- How much does it cost?

That's business planning in a nutshell.

Begin with what you already know about the proposed business. If you want to make widgets, what do you know about widgets? What do you know about making widgets? If there's a widget-making machine you'll need, figure out how you can get one and what it will cost. By listing what you know, you'll naturally isolate things you don't know.

What you don't know defines the research you'll need to do. For example, where do you get the raw materials for making widgets? What will it cost to power the widget-making machine? How much space will it require? Ask the questions; find the answers.

Fortunately, you can find excellent, reasonably inexpensive business-planning software on the market. The programs are wonderfully user friendly. They ask the questions, you fill in the answers and the program organizes the information into standard business plan format.

Business planning programs make it easy to do and redo your plan. Adjust this or that number and the program will quickly insert it and show you how it affects the overall plan.

A business plan largely focuses on the numbers—what, for example, it costs for office space, materials, equipment, etc. It's beyond important that you become a master of these. Learn to "recite your numbers." Nothing impresses the outside world more than an entrepreneur who has a clear grasp of the details of a proposed business.

It's not unusual to find that the numbers don't work your first time around the business planning cycle. But that's the beauty of business planning. When things just don't add up, you can start again and adjust the plan. Maybe you need to get the smaller widget-making machine, or locate the plant further out where rents are cheaper. Perhaps you should lease rather than buy the delivery truck. Or, saddest of all, maybe you can't make it work on the resources you have. Better to find that out now than after you've committed more time and money.

Once your business plan is finished, WORK THE PLAN! Make it your Bible. When you're caught up in the present, it's hard to plan for the future. The business plan does it for you. Trust your plan. Use it and rely on it.

.

If the office phone were supposed to be in place by such and such a date, make sure it's done. If your salesman is to move to straight commission in six months, make it happen. Follow the plan.

You were cool and calm and wise when you created the plan. Ignoring it once you open the doors is foolhardy. The business plan will help you keep emotional decision-making out of your business.

Your business plan reflects the wisdom of a calm, deliberative, research-based process. When you were creating it, you could see the big picture and understand how all the disparate pieces worked together to make it whole. Do you think you suddenly become wiser in the heat of battle? Apparently many small business people do because they trash their business plans at the first crossroads. When the bullets are flying is not the time to rewrite the battle plan. It's time to cling to it. It's time to steel yourself and work your carefully developed plan. It can be the difference between success and failure.

DISCIPLINING YOUR COMPANY'S FINANCES

Now, it's time to turn your business plan into an operating budget.

A budget is your company's financial road map. It's a mapping out of expenses and revenues for the year, and its math is ridiculously simple. If revenue is greater than expenses, you have a profit; if expenses are greater than revenue, you have a loss.

Both expenses and revenues need to be budgeted, but you should always budget expenses first. The reason is simple: You can control expenses, you can't control revenues. While you can research what things cost and decide what you want to spend, you can't make a customer walk through the door and buy. Revenue budgets are by definition a guess, because customer-buying decisions are out of your control. So, figure out what it will cost to run the business, and by default you'll know how much revenue the company will need to break even.

Budgeting to break even may not make you feel "tycoon-ish," but it will define the edge of the cliff for you. The likelihood of your first year's budget being dead-on falls somewhere between slim and none. Stay on top of the numbers, comparing your budgeted numbers with the actual numbers, and make adjustments accordingly. But, don't change the original budget. Instead, create an entirely new second budget, which reflects the reality of the situation.

If the actual numbers show revenues are not living up to what's needed for the business to break even, you need to adjust expenses, bringing them in line with the new reality. You need to do this regularly, with a new budget being created each time to adjust to what's actually happening on the ground. If expenses exceed revenues for the year, you'll have a loss. And losses cost real dollars. Your dollars.

Your business plan is a multipurpose document. In addition to using it as an overview of your entire business and as your budget road map, it can also be an excellent management tool. Don't miss the opportunity to use it for all three purposes. If you want to use it to help you manage, get your employees involved in budgeting. That works on both sides of the budget—expenses and revenues. If employees have input, they have "ownership" of the numbers; if they have ownership, they are more likely to want to make the numbers work. No longer do the numbers descend from on high to harass and hassle and make their lives miserable. Rather, the numbers become a common, agreed-upon goal to be achieved. Essentially, they will be reporting to the numbers and not to you. If tough adjustments need to be made, they'll understand why and accept it. After all, they missed their own targets. It's an effective and team-building method of management, and a way of treating your employees with respect. It may not be possible your first year, but from then on it will be.

SURVIVING AS LONG AS YOU CAN...

Sadly, a day may come when you finally decide the business just isn't working. Simply locking the doors and slinking away in the dark of night is no way to end it. Professionals always have an exit strategy.

James Bond, master spy, taught us you never enter a room without knowing how to get out. Likewise in business, never go in without knowing a way to get out.

Keeping your business agile, particularly in the early stages, can be its saving grace and/or your ticket to a graceful exit. In short, think short term. Lease instead of buy, and the shorter the lease the better. Though leasing may cost more, it keeps the business agile. If you discover to your horror that the location of your store is wrong, would you rather be holding a six-month lease or a deed of ownership? It may be cheaper to own, but it's tougher to disentangle in a pinch. Likewise, if the business doesn't succeed, which is easier and cheaper to walk away from? Buying is fine if the asset is a good investment and easy to dump if revenues go south. Otherwise, it's a commitment worth avoiding.

Likewise, avoid overstocking. You may miss out on quantity discounts, but the burdens of disaster will be lighter to bear. Long-term employment agreements are also unwise.

Agility is a small business's greatest advantage, allowing the business to respond quickly to opportunity and adversity. Keep the edge. Don't be mesmerized by the cheaper prices of larger buys and long-term commitments. They're more likely to fit your business like straitjackets than gloves. Let your business stretch and stay flexible. Being light on your feet lowers risks and lets you respond to changing situations. Keep your outlook short term—no more than a year.

Quitting is never easy, but done with dignity, it can bring respect. Call your vendors and let them know you're shutting the doors. They'll appreciate it. Getting the news from an automated voice, announcing the number they called is no longer a working number, has a sleazy sense about it. It rubs off on you.

Toughest of all is the prospect of re-entering the workforce. It's a humbling, pride-swallowing experience. You're no longer the owner or the boss. Steel yourself and do what you have to do. It's about survival—your survival. You took a shot and missed, nothing to be ashamed of there. Keep your head high and people will respond. *You* are not a failure, your business was.

No one likes to plan. It's tedious. It takes a great deal of patience. And it's all made up. But ask yourself: "If I don't have the discipline to plan, do I have the discipline to run a business every day?"

Commandment III: Thou Shalt Conserve Cash

New businesses don't run out of money, they run out of time to learn how to run a business and turn the money around.

Cash. Everybody wants it. Nobody has enough. Cash speaks of wealth and stability. It impresses and persuades. It feels good in the pocket and looks great in the hand. Its power is immediate and quantifiable. And unless you have piles of the stuff, it can occupy the mind inordinately because cash is central to our lives.

We work daily to acquire cash. Once we get it, we spend it sparingly and with great care, forever searching for "deals." We use it to live, to buy groceries and clothing and housing. We use it to avoid debt, so as not to incur interest. We're secretive about our cash, wanting no one to know how much or how little we possess. Regardless of all our myriad differences—race, creed, political persuasion and so on—we all love cash. But those are *personal* predilections concerning cash. In a business, cash's values and uses are altogether different.

CASH IS KING

If a business were a chess game, cash would be the king, the most powerful and mighty protector of the kingdom. The loyal subjects will do almost anything to protect the power of their king. The analogy fits because cash indeed protects a business during economic ups and downs and against unforeseen trials and tribulations. It makes much possible by its presence alone. It opens the doors and ears of the powerful, and opens minds to possibilities. Cash in a business is the asset extraordinaire.

In this chapter, we'll explore the power and uses of cash in your business. We'll talk of the imperative of putting aside your personal penchants to its uses and how to use cash to make your business go and grow. We'll also examine cash forecasting and connecting with its sources.

Make your money talk. People will listen.

USING CASH AS A STRATEGIC TOOL

Avoiding debt is not always a good business practice. It's not natural to think of debt as a positive thing, but you have to get used to it.

I realize your advisers have probably harped for years about the downside of debt, and here I am telling you it's not a bad thing at all, even a good thing. Whom to believe? The advisers? Or me? Listen to us both! We both know of what we speak. Your advisers are talking about you, the individual.

I'm talking about you, the business. They are different. The business "you" has to learn to think differently than the individual "you."

The business is its own self, with its own wants and needs, and its own healthy behaviors. Debt is one of those behaviors, even when it has the cash available to cover the cost of ... whatever. On a personal level, your instinctive caution concerning debt is wise. The credit card kind can cost a fortune and saddle you with years of payments. It smacks of living beyond your means. Some kinds of personal debt—car loans and mortgages, for example—are more socially acceptable. Still, you manage them very carefully.

Lenders, too, are cautious about extending the loan, checking carefully on your ability to pay the money back. Lenders, after all, are not in the business of lending, they're in the business of being paid back. They want proof of your income. They want to know what other debt you carry, and the history of that debt. Do you have a proven track record of paying your debts? Banks don't want to repossess the house or car you bought; they want to be paid back.

When lending to small businesses, and especially new small businesses, lenders rarely see a proven track record of income, and usually little or no assets as collateral. Any wonder you're not greeted with open arms?

A new business—less than three years old, say—has no proven track record of paying anyone back for anything. It has no collateral to offer because it has wisely avoided owning expensive, tangible assets. And bankers, in particular, know the failure rate of new businesses. How, then, can they justify lending the business money? They can if you have lots of cash.

A new small business with lots of cash and a solid business plan showing how long the cash will last has an apparent ability to pay back a loan. This makes banks more comfortable when making a lending decision. The adage is true: Banks will only lend you money when you don't appear to need it. And when you truly need it? Good luck. To exude the look of financial health, then, you should keep as much cash as you can in the business.

Never in the life of your business, for the foreseeable future at least, are you likely to have as much cash as you have on day one. That's an opportune time to try to borrow while conserving your cash. Don't worry about getting in too deeply; the marketplace will limit your borrowing appropriately, unless you do it with credit cards. Down that path lies trouble.

So, in business, cash is more than a possession, it is a powerful strategic tool, an asset to be conserved and exploited. While conserving your cash and exploiting it at the same time might sound like a contradiction, it's not. But the strategy requires great discipline and careful adherence to your budget. Your budget told you how much you could spend each month and on what. If you discipline yourself to live within your budget, you can do some decent cash management. If you don't pay attention to your budget, you can run out of cash before you know it.

When you begin to look into establishing credit relationships, you will quickly learn that banks are the least likely places to lend your small business money. Their hands are tied with regulations, but more importantly, the "risk-versus-reward" measurement nixes most small-business loans. The risks involved and the cost of managing the loan offset what they could make.

Leasing companies are more likely to lend you money than banks. And leases are the kind of financing that you need most often. To conserve cash, avoid spending large amounts of money on expensive assets such as equipment and real estate. Fortunately, leasing arrangements for this type of asset are readily available.

Take this example: If you brought $100,000 into the business and you immediately borrow $50,000 by leasing your equipment, you've increased your buying power by 50 percent. As a result of the loan, the financial position of your business is much stronger, even though it's taken on a monthly loan payment. If you had used $50,000 of your $100,000 to pay for the equipment, of course, you'd have no loan payment. But you'd only have $50,000 left for whatever else the business needs. Once your cash is invested, it's no longer available to cover payroll, for example. And, as your cash supply dwindles, it becomes harder to get credit. And when you can't get credit, there's only your cash—a vicious, business-sinking circle.

A healthy amount of cash on your balance sheet, combined with a reasonable amount of debt, demonstrates to the world that you know what you are doing.

Unlike in your personal life, when your business has cash, you want others to know it. In your private life, showing off how much cash you have in your pocket is both rude and dangerous. When you're at the checkout at the store and the customer ahead of you pulls from his pocket a wad of bills, lots of assumptions materialize. We conclude that the individual is wealthy, or perhaps that he is into something shady, but we always assume there's more where that came from. In business, "flashing" your cash is neither rude nor dangerous.

A healthy supply of cash on a balance sheet conjures images of stability and staying-power, which engender confidence. In the eyes of the credit-granting barons—banks or whomever— cash makes you a worthy and preferred customer. And the more cash you have, the worthier you are. That's how the system works. It's why cash conservation makes sense and why, unlike in our personal lives, keeping cash visible makes sense, too.

Projecting stability makes everyone we deal with more confident and willing to do business with us. Perception is reality. The more people you pay promptly, the more you get a reputation for paying your bills on time. To that end, the judicious spending of cash can make a world of difference. Getting into the habit of paying your small bills immediately encourages a positive belief in your business. So, examine your natural propensity to let the little guys go in favor of the big guys you fear. The little guys talk about you more than the big guys. And the little guys are desperate for your cash, just as you are desperate for theirs.

Managing your cash so it will last until the business is in a positive cash flow position is difficult. For most of us, managing cash is a short-term consideration. We get paid every week or two, so we make sure our money lasts until the next payday; that's the extent of our cash management skills. But in your business, you will need to manage your cash for months—until your business has a positive cash flow. Doing that without losing sleep every night requires you to adhere to your cash plan.

Trying to manage cash without paying heed to your cash flow budget is foolish. If you blow your cash too early, you can be out of business in no time. When your well runs dry, you have no other wells to draw on.

ESTABLISHING STRONG CREDIT RELATIONSHIPS

Face facts. You are probably not "bankable" when you start a business. Your sources of credit will be based on personal assets and will have nothing to do with your new business's potential. The time to start becoming bankable is at the very beginning of your business life. You do it by establishing credit relationships.

"Credit relationships," as opposed to "credit deals" or "credit arrangements," involve personal contact and are based on trust. Trust is an earned commodity, based on straight dealing and honesty. So, introduce yourself to a banker long before you ask for money. Form a friendly relationship in preparation for a credit relationship.

Bankers are a funny lot. They like things boring. They don't want to be "sold" on anything, having no wish to surf your wave of excitement and confidence. New, hot-from-the-hopper ideas frighten and discombobulate them. Balance sheets and income statements are their preferred reading. And a same-ol', same-ol' business approach makes them all warm and fuzzy. Believe me, if there were a "paint drying" channel, it would be on their favorites list. Be the paint, ladies and gentlemen, and you'll "wow" them to no end.

To a banker, excitement is more frightening than reassuring. You may be utterly certain your new business will boom, but keep the over-confidence under wraps; your banker won't appreciate it. A mini-Microsoft may be in your company's cards, but it's a journey you'll make one step at a time. Bankers want to know you know that. Realism means everything to them. To that end, make sure your published goals, as in your business plan, are attainable.

Outsized goals suggest a disconnect with reality. A business plan projecting $500,000 in revenues in year one had better spell out in convincing detail exactly how the revenues will be achieved. Anything less and you're more likely to be shown the door than the money. Realism is reassuring, particularly to the moneylenders. It suggests you understand the challenges of the task you're undertaking. Best of all, when you achieve or exceed those attainable goals, you'll inspire trust, which bodes well for the future of your relationship with your boring banker.

Sticking with your business plan is both wise and also a confidence-builder, from a banker's standpoint. Improvisation is a method of acting, not a method of running a business. Bankers know that, and when a business plan is marginalized, they get nervous. Staying the course is not boring, it's a good idea, and the bonus is it keeps bankers happy.

The bottom line when it comes to your banker—and financiers in general—is to stay under the radar. Establish patterns, toe the line, follow your plan and keep your nose to the grindstone. It's a lender-friendly modus operandi.

—

If you practice managing cash when you have some, won't you have more experience managing it when things are getting tight?

—

Commandment IV: Thou Shalt Sell Effectively

The business will not simply come to you. You have to give your prospective customers a reason to buy your product or use the service you offer.

Convincing customers they'd be better off with some of their money in your pocket is the long and short of selling. It's what business is all about. If you don't believe it, peruse a shelf in the business section of any bookstore. Half the titles will include the word "sales" or "selling." We're in business to make money, and selling products and services is how we do it. Stop selling and the business goes down. Thank heavens that selling is a skill you can learn.

Certainly, selling is an art. Surely, too, some of us are naturally better at it than others. But selling, like most of the arts, can be studied and learned. Selling is all about communication.

But fast-talking is not a requisite. In fact, the best selling is that which leads to repeat sales. You achieve that by making your customer feel good about buying from you.

Selling is also a science—a patient gathering of facts about people and products and how they interact. And it's an identifiable intellectual discipline—observation, hypothesis, test, conclusion. Common sense plays a role in selling, too.

In this chapter, we'll examine the art and science of selling. We'll talk about the intellectual discipline needed to be successful at it, and we'll explore best practices. We'll further examine advertising options and the importance of the Internet.

Selling effectively isn't the only thing, but it's a key to your overall success.

MARKETING INTELLECTUALLY, NOT EMOTIONALLY

His Grandma Becky was a great cook and the cuisine gene passed unspoiled to grandson Sam. His pastries were light, his meats succulent and his vegetables were to die for. "Sam's Dinners to Go" was a natural and he knew it. His perfectly prepared and packaged meals *made dinnertime a special time all the time.* Sam set up shop in an inexpensive place in Grandma Becky's old neighborhood. Gotta watch that budget!

In the paper and on radio, Sam shouted citywide the praises of his mouth-watering meals. But, though he built it, they did not come. Customers seemed singularly intent on giving Sam's Dinners to Go the pass. If only they'd give it a try, Sam thought, they'd be hooked, he was certain of it. But they just weren't trying. Sam was dumbfounded.

He shouldn't be.

Sam had made a classic mistake. He knew what *he* was selling—great food— but not what *they* were buying—convenience. He's got the emotional cart before the intellectual horse.

Sam was right as rain when it came to his cooking. It was knock-your-socks-off delicious, and he had a right to be proud. Problem was, his customers were buying convenience and Sam's Dinners to Go wasn't convenient. Grandma Becky's old neighborhood was way out of the way. They wanted good food, for sure, but they wanted convenience, too. Emotionally, Sam was selling his "art." Intellectually, he needed to be selling Sam's Dinners' convenience. In a nutshell, Sam didn't know the essence of his product.

The essence of a product is why customers buy it, and it's not always obvious. Sam's justifiable pride in his culinary capabilities was not the drawing card for customers. He needed to go after their schedules, not their taste buds, because his customers wanted easy, healthy dinners, first and foremost. It goes without saying that those dinners have to taste good. Understanding the essence of your product is the first step in effective selling. Understanding your product's competitive advantage is the next step.

A product's (or service's) competitive advantage is whatever sets it apart from the competition's product. It's what keeps customers coming back. In Sam's case, his competitive advantage was the scrumptious excellence of his dinners. Obviously, other businesses offer ready-made dinners to go, but Sam's simply tasted better. Their's tasted good, his tasted great. The essence of Sam's product remained its convenience, but its tastiness was its competitive advantage. He still needed to play to their schedules, but his gourmet gift would keep them coming.

Sam's mistake was in not understanding his customers' motivation. A more customer-friendly location would have helped his business succeed. Sam's choice of locations, though saving on rent, undercut his product's essence—convenience.

If he can't afford to move, the game will soon be over. Had he studied the competition, he would have learned the meals-to-go business is just like every other business: It's all about location, location, location.

Small businesses don't change the world. So don't try. The wheel has already been invented. Most successful small businesses copy the big guys, mimicking their successes and capitalizing on their failures. It's best to plug into an existing market because you don't have the time or money to change the culture. Focus your energies on understanding the world as it is and copy it as best you can. It's advice that holds true in nearly every aspect of small business, but particularly so when it comes to identifying your market.

Don't figure to find a better way. Don't rework the wheel and expect it to roll. To find your market, study the competition and copy copiously. Check out their stores and see who's buying what. Then learn all you can about them.

Knowing your customers is key: Where do they live? What are their buying habits? How old are they? What type of cars do they drive? Do they have children? Where do they congregate? If your customers frequent this part of town, don't put your store in that part of town, even though you always wanted a store there. Don't be like Sam. Learning about your customers and plugging into their flow is the goal. Be intellectual about it, not emotional.

Opening your wallet to hire a market research firm is unquestionably a viable option in the pursuit of market identification. But marketing research firms cost a lot of money and, truth be told, you can do almost as well on your own. Splurge on a $4 latte and park across the street from your competition. Count, take notes and observe. If it's important to know how many cars pass through a given intersection, spend a day or two sitting at the intersection and count them. If you'd like to know where your competitor's customers come from, ask. Not for addresses, of course, but ZIP codes. It's the kind of information that will help to direct your advertising.

Advertising isn't rocket science. Once again, it's a copy job. How is a product like yours normally advertised? Where? Know your customers and target them.

Advertise in fertile fields. If you know many or most of your customers come from a certain area, target that area with your advertising. It may be more emotionally satisfying to "explore" a new area, but where your customers are today is the most likely place that you'll sell your product or service. Compete in that area using your competitive advantage. Ever notice how competing businesses open up across the street from each other? If you feel you must plow new fields, do it carefully and know the "Fifty Mile Rule"—stay within fifty miles of home. In general a fifty-mile radius extending from your shop door to your customers is the limit for most small businesses. Any larger and you're pushing the envelope of your ability to adequately serve your customers. It gets expensive in dollars and resources to solve problems in a place you can't go to and return in less than a day. It may be sexy to open offices on distant shores, but it's risky, too.

LEARNING THE BEST SELLING PRACTICES

Modern marketing is amazing. Wander the aisles of a grocery store and study its layout. You can feel the mind behind it all. Products are grouped and positioned and ordered and displayed, all with one goal in mind—to get us to buy. Grocers have dissected and analyzed people's propensities and fashioned an environment that feeds off those propensities. And it works to near perfection. Every time we run into the grocery for a single item and come away with ten, we're proof positive of their marketing genius. Grocery stores know their customers.

In a nod to the notion that people are pretty much alike, learning your customers' buying propensities should begin with an analysis of your own buying habits. What draws you to products like yours—price, color, quantity? Whatever works with you likely will work with your customers, too. Figure it out—and go after them hard.

Remember, you need them more than they need you. Rare is the business that has customers beating a path to its doors. Yours is not the only shop on the block. Give them a reason to make your shop their choice for shopping. Stay one step ahead. Be smarter than your customers. Know your product, what makes it special and get the word out.

A second sale to the same customer is easier and less expensive to achieve than finding a new customer altogether. Choosing to do business with you a second time is an easier decision for a customer to make than was the decision to do business the first time around. Take advantage of that fact. Farm your customer base.

Gillette®, the creator of the safety razor, took a novel and somewhat counter-intuitive approach to converting customers from the traditional straight razor to their safety razor: It gave the razors away. The company was confident if you tried the razor you'd like it—and would need to buy blades from Gillette for years to come. The razor was the hook, the blades were the profit maker. It worked like a charm.

A promotion like Gillette's is just another form of advertising. The safety razor concept was new and the company believed strongly in its competitive edge. What better way to demonstrate the razor's advantage than to let people try it? An advertising blitz on radio—there was no TV at the time—

and in newspapers and magazines could have and probably would have worked fine. But putting the razor in the hands of customers sold them with more certainty than any advertisement, no matter how slick, could have done. Gillette was willing to think outside the box.

Creativity in promoting your product can win the day. Don't be afraid to be out front. Sure there are risks, but if you're careful, the rewards can be surprisingly good.

Again, copying your competitors is always a good idea. Here's a better one—go them one better. If you give customers a little more, they'll like it and likely patronize your business over the competition. Giving a bit more is nothing more than another advertising expense.

Capitalize on your strengths as a small business. Make it easy to buy from you. Make it fun to buy from you. Approach your customers as individuals, not as the masses. Promise more and deliver more. Knock yourself out.

Open your mind and don't be afraid. A misfire here or there pales in comparison to the hits you might create.

FINDING YOUR ADVERTISING BALANCE

Advertising pays. But it costs dearly, too. Finding cost-efficient methods of advertising that work is unquestionably important to the success of your business.

The effectiveness of any advertising is based on its ability to reach true potential customers, not on the sheer number of eyes and ears it reaches. Mailers that deluge a city may be seen by myriad eyes, but most won't have eyes for your business, so what's the point? Better to pay a bit more per pair of eyes (or ears) and reach those who have an interest in what you're saying. The increased response will more than cover the additional cost.

And then keep score. Tracking the response rate of each form of advertising you do is imperative. What worked for a time may no longer be working, or it may be working even better than before. Either scenario may suggest a change in mix of your advertising.

Trial and error in finding just the right mix of advertising is part and parcel of the game. Beware of long-term commitments, like the *Yellow Pages*. It's expensive and can't be adjusted once begun.

Big, expensive ad agencies may make you feel like a real player, but your bang-for-the-buck ratio won't necessarily reflect it. Big businesses don't pay much attention to small businesses because that's not where the money is for them. You need to work with people who need you as much as you need them. Small businesses tend to do best working with other small businesses. They're on the same wavelength. That's a real plus.

In an ad agency, large or small, you generally get relative to what you give. You know your product and its competitive advantage—they don't. You know your customers, too. Fill them in and they'll serve you better, though you might go away wondering why you needed them at all. Resist the feeling. They know their business and you don't.

WORKING ON YOUR IMAGE AND BRANDING

Hand me the chalk, I'm in the equation business:

$$B = CA + C$$
Brand = Competitive Advantage + Consistency.

Get the equation right and your business is home free, because your image and brand will say it all to customers:

"You know who I am. You know what to expect. You know my product will satisfy your desires."

A brand is the apex of marketing, essentially allowing your business to short-circuit your customers' thought processes. Most businesses never achieve branding. But for those that do, it's invaluable.

SBC®, one of the "Baby Bells" created when AT&T® was broken into pieces, turned around and acquired AT&T. After years of consciously cultivating the SBC brand, SBC tossed its name once the purchase of AT&T was completed. SBC is now at&t®. The reason is simple; AT&T's brand was better than SBC's—likely better than SBC's could ever hope to be. That's the power of great branding.

Competitive advantage is the basis of a brand, but its key is consistency. If your restaurant is known for thick and tasty milkshakes, you've got a brand with your customers. It will remain with you as long as you consistently deliver thick and tasty milkshakes. But let their quality slide and your brand will slide with it. A brand is a fragile thing.

Your logo is not a brand. Instead, it represents your brand. You want your logo to live up to your brand, not the other way around. If Anton Pavlov, the legendary behavioral psychologist, had a small business, his logo would make your dog salivate.

USING THE INTERNET

Remember the Fifty Mile Rule I spoke of earlier in the chapter? It doesn't count when it comes to the Internet.

Most people have never heard of Nesselrode pie. It was a delicacy on the East Coast in the '50s and '60s, but disappeared from the marketplace for some reason. I loved the rum-flavored meringue and flaky crust as a kid. In a conversation over lunch one day, I happened to mention it to someone who loves to bake. She said if I could get her the recipe she would bake me a pie. I did better than that. On the Net, I found that the exotic ingredients were available from a specialty store in Vermont. I ordered them, she baked it and the pie was outstanding.

Another time, I was searching for a particular old jazz record. I browsed the Net and found it on Amazon.com. When I received it, I discovered it had come from a small record store nearby. I knew the place existed, but would never have taken the time to go and rummage through its stacks.

Stories of Internet experiences abound. The Internet is the great equalizer, giving every small business the national and global reach of the big guys. And it's only beginning to flex its muscles. The Internet is here to stay. It's a huge opportunity. Take full advantage of it.

Every business should have a Website. Developing an effective Web presence is critical. Do it right. Make it a place worth a visitor's time. You don't need to spend a fortune, but don't cut corners either. It's an investment worthy of resources.

Make the site slick and fast, and fill it with information customers want and need. And be sure they can buy right on the site. Strike while the iron's hot. If customers are given only an ordering phone number to call, it's an extra step many won't take.

Amazon, eBay and similar buying and selling sites are also at your beck and call. Use them; they're filled with business opportunities.

Finally, get listed on as many search engines as you can. Search engines are a Web surfer's guide. They're your lifelines to customers. Learn all you can about them. Books on the subject are more than worth their cover price. Pick up one and read it.

Commandment V: Thou Shalt Negotiate Well

Negotiation skills affects what you buy as well as what you sell. Being an effective negotiator is crucial in turning a profit on the sales side and preserving financial resources on the consumption side.

It is good to be king. To be king is to be the ultimate boss of everyone. Say it and it shall be done. Request it and it shall be delivered. Demand it and watch them hup-two. Good, indeed! Kings don't have dinner—they feast. They don't flop on the couch for a nap—they retire to their chambers. Fawning attendants, stone-faced guards at every door, and a cadre of advisers to executive-summarize all the affairs of state. And subjects! All the twits and twerps to the far reaches of the kingdom are available for taxation.

Expendable riff-raff toiling tirelessly for the greater good—the king's comfort. Yes, it is good to be king.

But, alas, I shall never know its goodness. I am but a small-business man. No minions poised to do my bidding. No lackeys double-timing to satiate my desires. I have employees and customers and vendors—and negotiations. Always negotiations. But it's not so bad, for I've learned to negotiate well. So should you.

In this chapter, we'll examine negotiation. We'll explore strategies, like giving first and making the negotiating process win/win. We'll talk about the nitty-gritty of negotiating, identifying deal-breakers and thinking creatively. And, finally, we'll look at pricing policies, what's negotiable and what's not.

For all of us non-kings whose wishes are not commands, negotiating well is our next best option. Do it right and your business will become more peaceful. It's an art worth mastering.

Oh, by the way, before you start negotiating, make sure the guy on the other side of the table is the decision maker. Don't be trapped into negotiating something with someone who has to "check it with my sales manager" after you've played your best card. Except in very rare circumstances, if the person you're dealing with does not have the final say in the matter, don't waste your time.

DEVELOPING WINNING STRATEGIES

Given our druthers, we'd all like life to be "my way or the highway." Unfortunately, life doesn't work that way. Not even for kings. There are too many competing interests. We're left to negotiate what we want.

Negotiating is essentially about getting your way. Not in all its particulars, of course, but it is about getting what you need and as much of what you want as you can achieve in the process. That said, negotiation is not a competition. It's not about "beating" your opponent, though people often see it that way.

Most of us consider negotiating a game of power politics. Identify the leverage we possess over someone and threaten him or her with it. Do this or else. We flex power to win the day. Power is problematic, though. To begin with, it's temporary. Exhaust your power and you have nothing left. Secondly, if power is the ace, whoever holds the most aces wins—period. It's how dictators work. They hold the aces. They've got the power and you bow to it. If the guy across the table holds more aces than you, he'll take all he can and you'll make do with what's left. It's done in business all the time.

But small business is about the *lack* of power and the *lack* of leverage, so being a good negotiator becomes even more important. Besides, you have a better way to get what you want. It's called persuasion.

Practice the "art" of it all. The "art" in the negotiating process is to get others to do what you want because they want to do it! It's harder than simply playing power cards. It takes more patience and requires more skill. But the results are eminently more satisfying for everyone. No one feels bruised or beaten or taken advantage of. Your vendors, employees and customers—all people you negotiate with—will feel better about dealing with you. That makes for a more peaceful environment.

"Giving first" is a way to start down the right path. You disarm the other party early on by giving something without asking for something in return. Ideally, it's something you know the other party will appreciate. Instinctively, your counterpart will feel grateful and indebted to you. And you'll be seen as someone fair and reasonable to deal with. Your counterpart likely will be more pliant and more willing to "give" when the time comes. The strategy works with customers, too.

The baker who tosses in the extra cookie. The mechanic who tops off your antifreeze for no charge. These are forms of the "give first" strategy—small things to the small business owner, but important and appreciated things to you, the customer. Such simple gestures make you feel good and, by the way, more likely to do business with them again. Chinese restaurants have been doing it for years. Don't you miss the fortune cookie when it's not in the takeout bag?

Everybody knows a business is designed as a cold, money-making machine. By giving first, you inject a warm, human element. Customers will notice and respond.

As you enter into a negotiation, you certainly know what *you* need. But do you know what the person on the other side of the table needs? Knowing your opponent's needs is knowing where he is most vulnerable. Never forget: if you know someone's needs, you know his weaknesses.

The best negotiators understand their counterpart's situation. By understanding what your opposite absolutely needs, by default you know what he doesn't need. Those are the points on which you can make hay.

And how are you supposed to know what he wants? Listen and listen and then listen some more. Figure out how you can fulfill his stated "position" without compromising your own.

A friend created a video series for use in schools. When he sat down with a publishing house to negotiate a deal, he was fully prepared. He had researched the publishing business and had a working knowledge of its cost structures and associated risks. The publisher's costs and risks were upfront, associated with launching the product. My friend quietly accepted the low industry-standard royalty percentage. But he pushed for a sales trigger point at which his royalty percentage increased by nearly 50 percent, an unheard of increase in the publishing business. He got it, though. He knew if sales reached the trigger point, the publishers would not only have recouped their investment, but made a good profit, too. Beyond that point, any additional expenses they incurred would be made with little risk because they knew the series was selling. My friend understood what they needed to make their business work and where they could give.

Likewise, a vendor whose primary concern is getting paid on time will likely cut you a deal on price if you agree to pay him when the product is delivered. He gets what he wants and he's willing to "give" for it.

The best of all possible worlds, though, is when what he wants is what you don't want and what you want is what he doesn't want. That makes the negotiating process easy and satisfying. If you concentrate on meeting your opponent's needs, your needs will usually take care of themselves.

A good negotiation is not "won" by one party and "lost" by the other. A lot of tomorrows are yet to come. Your "win" may be ephemeral if the person who lost becomes particularly intransigent in future negotiations. Value your reputation as a fair dealer—and live up to it.

Cut a clean deal. Approach negotiation with a scalpel, not a meat ax. Don't create messes. Leave something on the table for your counterpart to claim as his own. You don't have to beat someone to win. Leave your ego at home. In a winning negotiation, both parties walk away pleased.

KNOWING THE ANGLES

Don't waste time. Negotiating is tough enough. Don't add to the difficulties.

Some things are negotiable, others not. If your counterpart has made it crystal clear that something is a non-negotiable point, don't bother asking for it. Not only are you wasting time, you won't get it anyway, and you're just interjecting frustration and negativity into the negotiations. In fact, if you are certain that something is absolutely not negotiable (not just a bluff), you might use this particular point as your "give first" item. He's not giving in on it anyway, so you might as well make some points and let him have it.

From your side, make sure you know in your heart of hearts what is and what is not negotiable for you. If your position *is* negotiable, don't pretend it isn't. I'm not suggesting you give away the store. But don't artificially and ridiculously stand your ground. You won't come across the hero who makes the huge concession to save the day by conceding on an important issue. If you've carried on about the absolute non-negotiable status of a point, then give in, you'll undercut your credibility and give your counterpart the upper hand. A non-negotiable point is a non-negotiable point. Period. Representing something as non-negotiable when it actually is negotiable makes you look like a game player rather than an honest partner trying to make a deal.

Sometimes a deal just can't be done, and no amount of good intentions or honest trying works. Don't contrive an arrangement just to complete a deal. Accept that you can't make it work and move on. Otherwise, you're only wasting time. "Natural" deals—those that evolve as discussions progress—are the only good ones.

Watch out for deal breakers. Viewed in isolation, deal breakers can verge on the petty and irrational. For whatever reason, a player gives outsized value to what seems a minor point. Don't try to make sense of it and don't be dismissive or insulting. You're dealing with something of value to him or her. Treat it as such and use it to your advantage.

Deal with deal breakers early on. Concede on the point or call it a day. Deal with it or it will taint the entire process. To hammer out the details of a deal and then see it sunk by a deal breaker is crazy. If a deal will sink, sink it soon and save yourself the time and hassle.

If it's a natural, make it happen. In a natural deal, the parties agree upfront on the general outcome and work together to fine tune the strategies so each will be happy in the end.

Sometimes you just know there's a deal in here. Find it. If you've been working together for years and it's been profitable and pleasant and both parties would like to see it continue, find a way to make it happen. When you hear of negotiations that have been going on for two years, that's generally what's happening. Both parties know there's a fit and are committed to finding it.

Be creative. Be clever. A good deal is worth the effort.

Negotiating is not a competition. You give a little, you take a little. If you don't accept that fact, you're not negotiating, you're just trying to win. And if you're merely trying to win, admit it to yourself and don't waste time negotiating. Just mail your opponent a contract to sign and say, "Take it or leave it."

A deal is made up of many little pieces interacting with each other to complete an arrangement. Home runs are not the only way to win a ball game. A string of singles can do the job just as well. Constantly swinging for the fences when negotiating can be more distracting than productive. It can blind you to the small things that can get you what you need just as well. There are many ways to cross the plate and each one produces a run.

ESTABLISHING A CLEAR PRICING POLICY

Few things are worse than discovering someone got the same car you just bought for $1,000 less than you paid. You feel humiliated, like you were taken for a ride. But that's how the automobile industry works—prices are negotiated. How does your industry work?

As with so many things in small business, the best strategy is to look to your competitors and copy them. If they have negotiable prices, you probably will have to have them, too. It's what your customers will expect. That's the industry standard. Conversely, if the industry standard is fixed pricing, you should go with fixed prices. Sounds easy enough, but things don't always work out that way.

Fixed prices aren't always so fixed. Some shop owners, thinking it's good marketing, will cut prices for their own customers, while requiring their employees to stick to the price list. Salespeople have it hard enough that everyone naturally wants to deal with the owner. Now customers have a monetary incentive to do so. So, they stand around and wait to speak to the owner while the salespeople who were hired to supplement the owner's own sales efforts sit idle.

I know a jeweler who went out of business because he always cut a deal for his customers and neutralized his salespeople. The store could not survive on his sales effort alone. If your prices are fixed, they should be fixed for everyone.

Losing a sale is tough. After all, isn't a negotiated sale a revenue producer? Perhaps, but more to the point: Is it a profit producer? A willingness to negotiate your "fixed" prices may indeed create more sales in absolute terms, and more revenues, too. But profits are what matter, not revenues. If selling at a lower "negotiated" price is not only good for gross revenue, but actually makes you a decent profit, why isn't the negotiated price the fixed price in the first place?

Customers learn the game quickly. When they smell blood, they strike. Once you negotiate prices, the sticker price no longer means anything. If your prices are fixed, keep them that way. You're asking for trouble if you don't. And you never have to be concerned if your customers talk to each other.

But if you use fixed pricing, how often can you change prices? That depends on how you publish your price list.

Fancy, four-color literature replete with pricing information looks great, but it's restricting because prices are only fixed until they change. If your business involves delivery and the price of gas doubles, your prices will eventually need to reflect that fact. Fancy printed price sheets are expensive to fix because they need to be reprinted, which may leave you with a closet full of out-of-date brochures. If you must create printed materials, keep them simple, basic and inexpensive.

Most of your suppliers have literature you can use to promote your products. They generally make it available for free or for a slight charge. Look into the possibility. You may save cherished advertising dollars on expensive brochures. Add your own computer-created price list and slip it into the vendor's materials. You'll have ultimate pricing flexibility and an attractive promotional tool.

Negotiating is a life skill. Haven't you gotten where you are by convincing other people of all kinds of things?

Commandment VI: Thou Shalt Serve Thy Employees

Good employees are hard to find. Lead by example and be the type of boss you would admire and like to work for.

The late, great management guru Peter Drucker built an illustrious career based on a simple insight: Dedicated employees are the key to successful companies. The idea seems so obvious, yet so few employers, large and small, get it. Too many people who intellectually grasp the idea forget it in the heat of battle.

Employees are merely extensions of their employers. Your challenge is getting employees to do what you want them to do, in the way you want things done. You can manage by being a leader or an adversary.

Sadly, many large organizations choose the adversarial approach. They play a power game marked by threats and poor communication. That's not a formula for a productive, creative, dynamic setting that brings out the best from employees. It's an atmosphere to be escaped.

The leadership approach is more demanding, but engenders loyalty and commitment in employees. Their well-being is a part of every decision. You make sure they have the tools and resources they need to do their jobs effectively. You communicate what you need from them and let them know where they stand. And you pay them before you pay yourself. Happy, confident, willing-to-work employees are the result.

So, how do you help your employees become contributing, reliable team members? Try treating your employees as if they were your children. Late night feedings and soccer game chauffeuring aside, if you want to know how to manage people, remember how you handle your children. This is not a condescending attitude. Good parents don't condescend to their children. Good parents recognize their role as shepherd, teacher and coach—exactly the traits of a good boss.

IF CASH IS KING, COMMUNICATION IS QUEEN

Employees need to be nurtured and taught. They want and need to know what is expected of them and how things should be done. Instead, employees are too often tossed into the fray poorly prepared and expected to figure things out on the fly. The successful boss will take the time to make sure employees are ready and able for whatever comes.

Employees want to know how and where they fit. They want to know who's the boss and to whom they report. They want to understand what authority they have. Letting employees know their roles and where they fit is the most important step in making them feel part of your team. (Incidentally, your organization chart should depict it all very clearly.)

Next, you have to face how much your employees need to know. Pull out your parenting skills again. What do you tell your kids about future plans or impending disasters? You can tell them everything, tell them nothing, or tell them what they need to know. The answer seems obvious: Tell them what they need to know (when they need to know it).

"Loose lips sink ships" may be an old adage, but it's still dead-on right. Information is power, and people like to flash it. If they have it, they'll pass it on, regardless of consequences. Telling employees everything is more than they, or the business, can handle. Yet sharing too much information is easy to do in the close-working atmosphere of a small business.

The flip side—telling employees nothing—is just as problematical. You're inviting insecurity, encouraging rumors and breeding distrust. In the absence of fact, people tend to make up their own explanations for things. Survival becomes all.

Employees need to know what they need to know, when they need to know it—and nothing more. Find the right balance and you'll allow your employees to do their jobs, feel secure and be part of the team.

So, there you have it, my contribution to the pantheon of managerial thought: Treat your employees as if they were your children. But don't get carried away. You will be the best boss if you seek your employees' respect before you seek their affection.

In this chapter, we'll explore employee management. We'll look at hiring and firing and rule writing. We'll also look at compensation strategies and benefit packages. (Benefits don't have to cost a lot, you know.) Finally, we will talk about employee turnover. (That does cost a lot.)

Open your mind and commit to being a good employer/ "parent." Your business will thank you.

DEVELOPING A HIRING AND FIRING STYLE

Hiring is an intimidating task—so important a call, so little to go on. A few short interviews, a one- or two-page resume, and it's decision time. Too much like a crap shoot. And if you blow it, you've got headaches and hassles and how-the-hell-did-I-make-that-mistake recriminations all round. Then comes firing time. Even worse!

Relax. Just pretend you're shopping. If you can shop, you can hire. You know what you need. You know what you can spend. You know what you expect from the product. Most of all, you know what you like and dislike. Keep those things firmly in focus and make your decision.

Here's a hint: Attitude trumps skill. You can teach skills, but mothers and fathers teach attitude. A potential employee may be brilliant and laden with skills, but if he's a drag on the environment, he's no kind of bargain, and your business doesn't need him. Skills get you nowhere if you can't get along with others. Of course, if it's an electrician or a plumber or an architect you need, the requisite skills are a must. But never short-sell attitude. A bad attitude is like a malignancy, infecting and spreading to all it touches. The close-knit environment of a small business makes it doubly destructive.

So, shop until you find what you're looking for. Trust your instincts. Don't be afraid to make the call. You have no boss from on high picking at your decision. You're the boss.

Of course, we'd all love a magic crystal ball to divine the inner workings of prospective employees. But as much as you'd love a little peek inside the hearts and heads of potential hires, you must respect their privacy. Trying to delve too deeply is strictly out of bounds. Laws limit what you can and can't ask, and people are aware of them. Know the laws and follow them. If you wouldn't ask it of a total stranger, don't ask it of an interviewee. Showing respect in an interview sets a good tone for any future relationship you and the potential hire may have.

Unfortunately, hiring is an inexact science. Sometimes you will make the wrong call. So, as dying is part of living and losing a part of winning, firing is part of hiring.

Firing someone is hard not just on you and the employee being fired, but on everyone in the office. Your firing style is as important as your hiring style. Do it poorly and you undermine office cohesion, maybe irretrievably. There are books on firing. You'd be wise to read one.

First and foremost, understand that you share a good deal of the responsibility when employees are fired. You hired them. Their training was up to you. You provided their work environment. At one time you thought they were the right people for the job. What happened? Some introspection and soul-searching are in order. Learn and grow and improve from the situation. Become a better "parent."

Next, understand that just because the employee didn't work out for you doesn't mean the person's no good. Your stars didn't align as you hoped. There's no shame to anyone in that. Things just didn't work out. Leave the person's dignity intact. Be sensitive to his or her feelings.

"Never do anything in anger" is a rule to live by, particularly when firing someone. Don't wait until you're about to erupt. Unless the firing was for "cause"—stealing, drugs or some other cataclysmic event—you should see it coming. Don't let it get to the boiling point. Explosions send shrapnel in every direction. Innocent bystanders suffer. When signs of problems first appear, let the employee know and work with the person to fix the problem. You need to look the employee in the eyes and say you're not pleased.

Employees need to feel they got a fair shake. They might never want to admit it, but in their heart they'll know if they got what they deserved. And so will their fellow employees. You're playing a difficult scene to an audience—your other employees. They'll appreciate it if your performance is worthy of a "People's Choice" award.

ESTABLISHING CLEAR AND SIMPLE POLICIES

People like rules. Clear, simple, easily understood rules are their support and comfort. If they understand the rules, they understand how to "win." A clearly understood system of reward and punishment is the key.

Your objective is to create an efficient, cohesive, pleasant work environment. Any rules and policies you create for the company should be measured against that yardstick. Look at each rule and policy you've initiated and ask yourself how it helps to achieve your objectives. Requiring coats and ties in an office where clients and customers never come is pointless. Requiring prompt attendance by 7:30 a.m., because that's when calls start coming in, makes sense.

Be prepared to live by the rules you create. A set for them and a set for you and "ne'er the twain shall meet" is not an option. You may be first among equals, but when it comes to policies and rules, you're just an employee. And as the leader, you need to set a good example. An added benefit to living by your own rules is you'll be less likely to create irritating, nit-picky ones!

Avoid petty rules. You know what they are because they annoyed you as an employee. They're rules that smack of Scrooge before his Christmas-eve conversion, rules for the sake of rules, rules that disdain people's lives beyond work— no personal phone calls, forty-five-minute lunch hours, no doctor's appointments on work days.

Treat people like adults and they'll act like adults. If people begin abusing the rules or taking advantage, a simple warning, or even a slight tightening of the rules, is always possible and will get the message across. People know when they've gone too far. Again, it's just like parenting.

A good system of rules and policies defines the working environment. But a well-defined environment is not necessarily a pleasant and productive one. Once you've set the ground rules, you need to concentrate on the factors that can cause employees to *want* to work for you, rather than for someone else, and cause them to be excited and productive at work.

Aim for a bright, cheery, safe, comfortable environment. Decent lighting, comfortable chairs and clean restrooms help make an office a pleasant, inviting place. Dirty, dark and dreary create the dread of a prison block. Which do you think inspires productivity?

Let employees know you recognize that they have lives beyond work. When they don't feel squeezed between work and home, employees are better at both, and happier to boot. A bit of flexibility that recognizes their balancing act never hurts. People want to do well and be good employees. Letting them breathe and balance their lives is their ticket to achieving it.

UNDERSTANDING BENEFIT AND COMPENSATION PLANS

You need to offer your employees benefits. Now, take a moment, wipe the cold sweat from your forehead and read on. You can do it. Really.

As in most things business, bang-for-the-buck should be your guiding principle when selecting and designing company benefits. Start from the standpoint of what your employees need, not what you can afford, and you're on the right path.

Small businesses are in a better position than larger companies to offer small, family-friendly benefits, simply because they have fewer employees. Take advantage of your smallness because little things, with incidental costs to your business, can make people feel you have a great place to work. For example, a day off on birthdays or other significant days is a surprisingly prized benefit. Flowers or dinner on you for wedding anniversaries is another idea. Try sponsorship of a soccer team or a monthly drawing for a Friday off. Be creative. Good benefits—particularly those that plug into employees' lives—are part of an overall management strategy. The more benefits you offer, the less your employees will look at their monetary compensation as their only reward.

Flextime is an example. Employees can blend the worlds of work and home with less stress and hassle—a benefit with impact that costs nearly nothing. And it's an area where small businesses have a decided advantage over big companies. Arriving at 7 a.m. and leaving at 4 a.m. can make a world of difference to employees with kids in day care, and the impact on the office is likely minimal. A laptop computer, which will make work at home possible when duty calls, will do wonders for sanity all around. You've got a family. You know the demands. Make the business as flexible as possible to your employees' needs. Each conflict you conquer will improve productivity and loyalty.

Certainly, "traditional" benefits are costly, but don't ignore them. Health insurance costs are already high and are rising quickly. Even large, established companies are bending from the weight. Still, you can offer a group plan to your employees. As a business, you can offer group insurance. Just because you make it available doesn't mean you have to pay any of the premiums. Your employees may need to pay 100 percent of the premiums, but at least they'll have a group. Likewise, with retirement plans. You don't need to provide a matching contribution, just provide a plan your employees can contribute to. Your competitiveness in the marketplace as an employer is enhanced simply by offering the benefits. And don't stop there. Put your imagination to work. Little things like intra-company competitions, special parking spaces and theme days can make your place the fun place.

Compensation is a management tool. Either pay people properly or don't employ them. There's no need for extravagance, but squeezing employees just because you can, or because you're cheap, is truly counter-productive. If an employee is not performing up to snuff, fire him and find someone else. Cutting his pay or denying him raises will do nothing to improve the quality of his work, and will likely poison the atmosphere. If he's not right, he's wrong. There's no middle ground. If an employee is not worthy of an annual pay raise, why is he or she on your payroll?

A dead-end job is a dead-end job, and stagnation is not inspiring. Structure each position so that it offers an expectation for future improvement. Even a dishwasher can be promoted to busboy. Give employees an incentive for hanging in there, and give yourself the ability to reward good work.

Even a small business has ways to keep employees working toward goals. Keys to the office, business cards, personalized note pads are all ways to reward employees and show recognition for achievement. Be creative.

Incentive compensation and bonuses can be effective management tools, but they are rarely used correctly. They should be enticements to push achievement to the very edge. With these, you're enticing your employees with the carrots of incentive pay and bonuses to get them to achieve something above and beyond the norm. If incentive pay and bonuses are not tied to clearly defined, effort-stretching goals, you're wasting your money. Routine job activities are compensated for by regular pay. Special compensations like incentives and bonuses are for "special" achievements. They are not part of "normal" income, though many employers have fostered that notion by awarding incentives and bonuses that are not connected to a successful "special" effort. Set a goal—ideally in concert with the employee—and give the employee the incentive to achieve it. Make the challenge positive. Doing so keeps the incentives and bonuses fresh, special and worth going after.

Now, let's talk about your compensation structure: If you're paranoid about your employees finding out what the other guy makes, that's a sure sign things are out of whack. If posting everyone's pay arrangement on the backroom bulletin board would cause a revolution, it's time to review your salary structure. In a small company, everyone's likely to know the gory details anyway. If things are not fair, and you would be embarrassed (or worse) if the facts were known, better put them in order. Inequitable pay structures are time bombs that usually go off at the worst possible time. Unfair pay relationships happen because the squeaky wheel gets the oil. Do yourself a favor and keep the whole machine properly lubricated.

LIMITING EMPLOYEE TURNOVER

Serving your employees boils down to keeping them happy and on-board. Your goal is to avoid turnover—the most expensive thing you'll encounter in employee relations.

A key to avoiding turnover is to make your employees feel secure. Communicate. Communicate. Communicate.

Employees who know where they stand don't waste time worrying about their status. That's information they can only get from you. If their work is "A" quality, let them know. If it's "B" quality or worse, let them know, too—and how they can correct it. They may not like the grade but at least they know. Knowledge in this instance is comfort. Keep them in the dark, and they'll assume the worst. One common tactic employees use to find out how they're doing with you is to ask for a raise. If they don't get it, they know the truth. Making them ask for positive feedback in the form of a reward to determine their job security is a sad state of affairs. Don't make them ask. Tell them regularly how they're doing. It's how your relationship with them should work.

People respond well to fairness. They may not like everything you decide, but if like actions bring like consequences for everyone, you'll get few complaints. No one expects you to be chummy with your employees, but everyone expects you to be just.

Sometimes in employee relationships, one party or the other wants guarantees. The dynamic of the relationship is spelled out: If I do this, you'll do that. Most often the guarantee takes the form of an employment contract.

Most of us prefer guarantees. Unfortunately, employment contracts often have a subtle, undermining effect on effort and initiative. We hunt with less diligence when hunger's not lurking. We don't push or go the extra mile. Beware of employment contracts. In small businesses, they diminish employer and employee alike because, at heart, they're an admission of a lack of trust between the parties.

If putting things in writing is the only way the employer/employee relationship can work, that's a problem. Employment contracts restrict mobility. And mobility is everything to a small business. Consider employment contracts carefully. Unless there is clear benefit to both parties, don't sign.

Non-compete agreements are legitimate tools to protect a company. While you work for me, you'll have access to sensitive and proprietary information and client lists. When you leave, you cannot take that information for your own or anyone else's use. Fair enough. But be very, very careful. An improperly drawn agreement may be unenforceable. Never try to prepare a non-compete agreement without the help of a lawyer with experience in that area.

The employer/employee relationship works best with honest, straightforward communication. Be consistent. Keep things under control. Volatility and broad swings of temperament make people feel insecure.

The best way to keep people from leaving is to make them want to work for you. If you serve their needs, they'll serve yours.

Ideas are dime a dozen. No one ever got rich on an idea…they got rich by executing an idea. Can you do it alone?

Commandment VII: Thou Shalt Obey the Law

Be careful in all of your business dealings.
Consult an attorney whenever in doubt.

"*You gotta know the angles.*"
"*It's not what you know, it's who you know.*"
"*Smart people never invest their own money.*"
"*Pay yourself first and everyone else second.*"
"*Never sell anyone anything without making a profit.*"

Do you know what all these pieces of common business wisdom have in common? They're all crap. People who disseminate them believe the way to financial nirvana is to use the easiest way you can find. Not the plodding, smart, experienced, difficult way. Not the legal, considerate, decent, "I-sleep-well-at-night" way.

Don't succumb to the supposed "easy" way. It's the best way to be in business for a short time. If you want to be in business for the long term and spend your money on growing your enterprise, rather than on settlements and legal fees, learn the rules and stay within them.

The key phrase to remember is, "Ignorance of the law is no excuse."

In this chapter, we'll examine the law as it applies to small business and the importance of following it to the letter. We'll explore your rights and obligations under the law and the need to stay properly licensed. And we'll discuss employment law.

"Laws are made to be broken" may have a clever ring and a charming bravado, but it's a road to ruin. Play by the rules. Follow the law.

KNOWING YOUR RIGHTS AND OBLIGATIONS

Every business transaction consists of two parties, a buyer and a seller, creating a contract between them, whether written or not. As with any contract, each party is empowered with certain rights and responsibilities. Rights and responsibilities are the two sides of the legal coin. Your rights are a reflection of the responsibilities of others, while your responsibilities reflect the rights of others. Business law simply codifies those rights and responsibilities.

A handy rule of thumb for most situations is the "reasonable man" test. "What could a reasonable man rightfully expect in this situation?" Answer honestly, and you'll generally know if what you want to do is legal or not. Another good guide is your gut. If something feels right, it's probably legal. If not, it's probably not legal. We all have a sense for what's right and wrong, learned at our mother's knee. Listen to it.

You're most in control of your responsibilities to others. Delivering the product you advertise is an obvious responsibility. Living up to your promises is another. That's not only a legal requirement, that's good business. Baiting and switching, on the other hand, isn't good business—and it is illegal and unethical as well.

Contracts go both ways. You have rights, too, and knowing what you're entitled to is your best defense against settling for less. Creating and posting a merchandise return policy will help keep customers from taking advantage of you. The most expensive dress shops usually require returned dresses to have their original tags attached and intact. Such policies were fashioned in direct response to customers who bought dresses and wore them to an event, then tried to return them as unused. (Would someone do such a thing?) Not surprisingly, tags are fastened conspicuously.

Customers also have the responsibility not to cheat you. Writing bad checks or using invalid credit cards are obviously illegal. Establishing appropriate safeguards and procedures—not accepting personal checks, for example—is an excellent way of protecting yourself, and is clearly within your rights. That's far better than chasing deadbeat customers through the courts.

But perfect protection doesn't exist. Do your best and pick your battles carefully. The legal system is an expensive solution.

UNDERSTANDING THE LAW AS IT APPLIES TO YOU

Legal documents are a fact of business life. Leases, sales contracts, employment agreements and warranties are just a few you'll likely run across. They can be cumbersome reading, but they're not written in Greek. A helpless, glassy-eyed stare is not an acceptable response. Remember: Ignorance is not a legal defense. Always get appropriate legal help before signing anything, but also have a clear understanding of basic legal documents yourself. It's not rocket science.

An important aspect of doing business in this country is the "Uniform Commercial Code" (UCC). The set of laws was mutually agreed upon by all the states to facilitate trading. The code governs all commercial transactions in the country. You must have a working knowledge of the UCC as it applies to your business. In fact, you should aim to possess a lawyer's knowledge of the UCC as it applies to you and your business.

Specialized local laws also require your attention. If you're a restaurateur, know the health codes like the back of your hand. Getting slapped with a violation can be expensive, and it could kill your business. Don't make compliance a guessing game. Good intentions don't count. Whatever your business, know the codes that apply to you.

Everything you sell comes with a warranty. By selling a customer a widget, you warrant that it will do what widgets are meant to do. If a reasonable man could rightfully expect a widget to work in a certain manner and your widget doesn't, you're in trouble—maybe serious trouble. The fact that you didn't realize widgets were used in that manner is no excuse. If your product has unacceptable uses, clearly disclose that fact in your literature.

Understanding the law as it applies to your business sounds more daunting than it really is. Laws rarely change. Once you learn them, you needn't subscribe to a legal update service to stay current. Basic business law is basic business law. The cost of a book on the subject (one of the "Dummies" series perhaps) is exponentially cheaper than the legal fees you will incur if you are in violation. Furthermore, laws tend not to be difficult to obey. The legislative process is so filled with debate and compromises, the final product is usually comfortably broad and reflects the practical aspects of the circumstance being governed.

So, within this broad area of allowable activity, you usually have plenty of room to maneuver. Generally, stay away from the edges of law, lest you go over. You have little to gain and much to lose.

STAYING PROPERLY LICENSED

Chances are your business is small enough not to appear on any radar screens. Your gross income, the number of employees and the square footage you occupy are tiny enough not to attract anyone's attention. Anonymity is a good thing. It means no one will hassle you. It means that the authorities barely know you exist. Keep it that way. Stay off the legal radar screen.

ILLEGAL BUSINESSES ATTRACT ATTENTION SO STAY LEGAL

One easy way to have the full force of the law come down on you is to be sloppy with your licenses. Make sure your licenses are current! An expired business license is attention-getter number one, and license inspectors don't play around. Muscle-flexing is their favorite pastime.

Government's first duty is to protect the public, and officials take the job seriously. Licensing businesses is one way they do it. Your business is part of their database and they know when your license is due. Make sure you know, too—and keep current. Doing so is easy and inexpensive.

Licenses don't cost thousands of dollars, they cost tens of dollars. Depending on your business, you may need federal, state and local licenses. If you're hauling waste, the EPA probably has a license you need. Find out. Don't let yourself become illegal. It's a sad and senseless way to fail. Learn the rules and follow them.

LEARNING THE BASICS OF EMPLOYMENT LAW

Learn to know employment law well and to get appropriate advice.

A common mistake small-business owners make is labeling an "employee" a "subcontractor" or an "independent contractor." The lure is savings: An employer avoids Social Security costs and unemployment taxes when dealing with subcontractors. That's about a 10 percent savings. People who play this angle think they're "clever" business people. Believe me, it's not worth it. Inappropriately treating an employee as a subcontractor violates federal law—never a good idea.

The Internal Revenue Service has a list of questions to determine employee versus subcontractor status. Get a copy of the list and answer the questions with brutal honesty. If there's a sliver of doubt, the person is an employee. That's the way the system works. The reality is, other than outside professionals, almost everyone you work with is an employee. Fundamentally, people are employees unless they do the same thing you're paying them to do for a variety of other people, at their own discretion, using their own judgment when doing their job.

Learn the rules of hiring and firing. Both are full of pitfalls. Some people make money by bringing suits against employers who make innocent hiring and firing errors out of ignorance. Find a good book on hiring and firing rules and regulations. Sounds like a dull evening for sure, but you'll find the time well spent. Hiring and firing have too many nuanced "can't-do's" for you to simply wing it. If you don't know the letter of the law, and someone is determined to hold you to it, you'll lose.

When hiring, treat prospects with the utmost respect and ask no personal questions. Not their age, marital status or whether they're pregnant or have plans to become pregnant. Study their resumes carefully and you can discover the answers to most personal questions anyway—just don't ask them.

Firing is the more troublesome gamut to run. Discrimination is a minefield in itself. Age, race and gender discrimination cast a pall over every firing. Be careful. If it looks like discrimination, even slightly, tread lightly. Don't be afraid to get the advice of a labor lawyer. Up-front legal fees are a lot cheaper than settlements after the fact.

**The legal arena is not a comfort
zone for most of us. Do your homework
and seek advice whenever you're
not absolutely sure.**

Commandment VIII: Thou Shalt Keep Excellent Records

Always back up your business transactions and activities with solid record keeping. Whether its paperwork or digital files always back it up or make copies for off-site storage.

The only perfect game in World Series' history was pitched by Don Larsen in 1956—a 2–0 gem that saw not a single Brooklyn Dodger reach base. Wish I had been there. Alas, I was doubly doomed—tickets were scarce and infants didn't get to go to the World Series. Yet given a completed scorecard from that milestone, I could reconstruct the game, batter by batter, out by out, inning by inning, as if I had occupied a box seat behind the Yankee dugout, popcorn and Crackerjacks filling my cheeks. Baseball is rife with record keeping. In your business, be like a baseball scorekeeper— keep excellent records.

In baseball, keeping records is a passion. In business, it's the law. When tax time comes, and it always does, your records will see you through. If you don't have them going in, they'll have to be created. That's a costly process. The need for records doesn't go away because you ignore it. The job only grows bigger … and bigger … and—you get the picture.

In this chapter, we'll look at record keeping. We'll examine why good record keeping is important for your business, explain "the books" and compare and contrast bookkeeping and accounting. We'll also explore ways to avoid being financially victimized. Finally, we'll review basic financial statements.

Few of us went into business to bean count, but it's part of the game and a valuable part at that. Be not afraid. Resistance is futile.

ACCEPTING THE IMPORTANCE OF RECORD KEEPING

When someone asks me "What should I have done—made that late night sales call or completed my paperwork for the day?" my answer is "Yes." That generally stops the questioner cold, but "Yes" is the only answer. Both need to be done.

Doing your paperwork ranks right up there with making sales. No rule says you must prepare your records personally, but the rule says they must be prepared. Don't run from them. The books won't vanish if you neglect them. They *will* get their due. The question is how difficult or expensive do you want the task to be.

I've had a lot of "shopping bag" clients over the years. Those are people who show up at my door, embarrassed and helpless, carrying twelve months' worth of receipts in a shopping bag. They plead for redemption from their sin of "never getting around to it." They swear their intentions had been good, but their days had been exhausting and at 11 p.m. at night, when they meant to get it done, they needed their pillow, not paperwork. Don't kid yourself. A lack of motivation defeats good intentions every time. Don't a shopping bag client be!

Covet good records. They're an excellent navigational tool. To understand where you have to go, you need to know where you've been. Before the year began, you created an operational budget for the business. The books and the various financial reports drawn from them will let you know how you've fared at year's end. Maybe you're winning big. Maybe not. The information is real and revealing and can help you adjust, track and fine-tune your course.

Besides, keeping books is not an option. It is a legal requirement. The feds are doubting Thomases unlike you've ever seen. You claim it, you better be able to prove it. At tax time, your books are your best friend. Treat 'em right.

Everyone's Books

SALES
Invoices
Credit Memos

CASH RECEIPTS
Deposit Slips

PURCHASES
Vendor Invoices
Debit Memos

GENERAL LEDGER

CASH
DISBURSEMENTS
PAYROLL
Checks Issued

GENERAL
Reserved for
your accountant

Keeping books is not hard. "The books" are nothing more than numerical diaries. Accountants actually refer to them as "journals." Something happens, you write it down. You deal with six books: Five are "books of original entry," called the journals, and one is the "book of final entry," called the ledger.

Did you buy something, sell something, pay for something or get money for something? Answer that question and you'll know in which of the five books of original entry to record a transaction—in the **sales journal**, the **cash receipts journal**, the **purchases journal** or the **cash disbursements journal**. We call them books of original entry because you record original transactions in them. Each month, each journal is tallied and the totals are recorded in the fifth book, the **general ledger**, a summary of the journals. A fifth journal, the **general journal**, like the general ledger, is only used by your accountant. The general journal fixes errors in the other journals and makes special accounting adjustments at the end of an accounting period.

While larger companies might have additional books and often don't call them journals, that's what they really are. They're merely specialized subdivisions of the five books of original entry. Most businesses also prefer to break the cash disbursement journal into two separate books, one for normal cash disbursements and one for payroll. But a set of books is a set of books, whether it's your company or General Electric. The principles of record keeping and double-entry bookkeeping are universal in business.

I am often asked, "If I have a bookkeeper. do I need an accountant?" and vice versa. Again, the answer is "Yes." You need a bookkeeper every day and an accountant periodically. Most bookkeepers are not trained accountants. A bookkeeper records company transactions in the journals, while an accountant audits the books and creates documents revealing their contents to the outside world. A company can live without a bookkeeper, but not without an accountant.

Bookkeepers process all the company paperwork. They open the mail, prepare the journals and, with the help of accounting software, post the general ledger. In addition, they usually take care of all other office functions no one else wants to do. It's an important position, but because of the straightforward nature of most accounting software, it is not one that's beyond the abilities of most employees if given a bit of training.

Accountants, on the other hand, should be college trained in their expertise. Accountants audit the books for accuracy and make sure the books comply with generally accepted accounting principles, or GAAP. GAAP compliance is critical because financial statements, which communicate the company's financial health to the world, are derived from information from the books. Investors, bankers, vendors and all others who have an interest in knowing the financial status of a business need to know the statements they see were created in accordance with accepted accounting rules. Otherwise the statements are of no value.

PREVENTING THE TEMPTATION TO STEAL

Over the years, I've been involved in many embezzlement audits. I do these when someone suspects that funds have been misappropriated. Essentially, I reconstruct the books to trace the wrongdoing. Today, it's called "forensic accounting." In almost every instance, the business itself was complicit in the theft. They were not co-embezzlers, but rather the powers-that-be who didn't have a system of fundamental business controls in place. Their negligence made the embezzlement possible.

I've also learned that most embezzlements are serendipitous. People are basically honest. Rarely do they wake up one day and decide to become thieves, setting their minds to figuring ways of robbing their employers. Nine times out of ten, they fall prey to repeated temptation. One day, it simply gets the better of them.

Case in point: A young woman was charged with making the daily deposit of cash receipts. She did so religiously for years. Then one hectic day, she truly forgot to do it. Lo and behold, nobody at the company noticed. No one was crosschecking or even reviewing bank statements. A week later, she "forgot" on purpose and started to make a habit of it. Eventually, she got caught. Certainly, she was guilty, knew better and had no right to do it—shame on her. But shame, too, on the company for dangling that temptation before her.

Basic controls are simple. If your business uses cash registers, balance them every day. Make sure what's supposed to be in the register is in fact in the register. Whoever opens the mail should not also do daily bank deposits. Lock what should be locked and don't give everybody keys. Sign checks personally. If you can't, have them double-signed. That way, the signers would have to be in collusion to steal—this is far less likely to happen. Don't tell everybody everything. Don't get sloppy.

All that said, don't be paranoid, either. Employees expect and understand controls and checks and balances. Go too far, get too nit-picky, and the message you deliver is that you don't trust them.

By the way, without good records, you'll never even know if you're being robbed.

GETTING COMFORTABLE WITH FINANCIAL STATEMENTS

Financial statements are really not hard to understand, and you need to know how to discuss them. Financial statements are created from the general ledger. The general ledger, as we've discussed, is a summary of the five journals. Your business has three basic financial statements—the balance sheet, the income statement and the statement of cash flow.

Balance Sheet

ASSETS	LIABILITIES & EQUITY
Current Assets	*Liabilities:*
Convertible to cash	Current Liabilities
within 12 months	Payable within 12 months
	Long-Term Liabilities
	Payable in more than 12 months
Fixed Assets	*Equity:*
Capital assets and land	Capital Stock
	Retained Earnings
Other Assets	
Everything else	

A **balance sheet** is a snapshot in time, a picture of your business at a particular moment. A balance sheet has two sides, *assets* are one (the left side) and *liabilities and equity* is the other (the right side). Like the name says, the two sides need to balance. Ergo, assets = liabilities + equity, which happens to be known as "the fundamental equation of accounting."

Pretend you just bought a house for $200,000, having put down $40,000 and borrowing the $160,000 balance. On a balance sheet, on the asset side, the house would be listed at a value of $200,000, or what was paid for it. On the liabilities and equity side, your liability, or what you owe on the house, would be listed as $160,000, and your equity, or what part of the home you've already paid for, would be listed as $40,000. *Voilà!* The balance sheet is in balance with each side adding up to $200,000. Your assets equal your liabilities plus your equity.

On your company's balance sheet, assets are divided into three basic categories: current assets, fixed assets and other assets. *Current assets* are things convertible into cash within twelve months—cash itself, accounts receivable and inventory, for example. *Fixed assets* are things not convertible into cash within twelve months—buildings, land, heavy equipment and such. *Other assets* are pretty much anything else that doesn't fit into the other two categories. Your business will probably not use this category.

The right side of the balance sheet lists company liabilities and company equity. Liabilities are broken into two sections—current liabilities and long-term liabilities. *Current liabilities* are those due within twelve months, while *long-term liabilities* are those with maturities longer than twelve months. The equity section is simply the difference between your assets and your liabilities.

Now let's talk about financial ratios. Ratios are a way to analyze and interpret your balance sheet. A ratio is the relationship between two numbers on the balance sheet. A frequently used ratio is the *current ratio*—the ratio between current assets and current liabilities. It is the measurement of how likely you are to have the cash to pay your current liabilities. A good current ratio is two to one—two current assets for every current liability.

Another popular ratio is *debt to equity*—total liabilities divided by equity. It is the measurement of how much of your assets you actually own outright. Point-five to one will get you by. In other words, you owe fifty cents for every dollar you have invested. This is quite conservative, but it's healthy for an early stage business. Simply stated, this ratio shows who has more invested in your company—you or your creditors.

You've heard the term *working capital*—that's current assets minus current liabilities. You're measuring how much money you have to "work" with to run your business if you paid off all of your current liabilities.

That's it. That's a balance sheet. Not Greek at all, is it?

Income Statement

REVENUE
    Sales
COST OF GOODS SOLD (Costs directly related to the stuff you sell)
    Purchases
    Direct Labor
    Supplies
        GROSS MARGIN
SELLING EXPENSES (Costs of bringing in business)
    Advertising and Promotion
    Commissions
GENERAL & ADMINISTRATIVE EXPENSES (Costs of running the back room)
    The Fortune You Make
    Everything else
OTHER INCOME AND EXPENSE
    Interest Income
    Interest Expense
        NET INCOME BEFORE TAXES (What's left before Uncle Same takes his cut)
TAXES ON INCOME (Only if you're lucky)
    Federal and State Taxes
        NET INCOME (The bottom line)

Now let's look at its companion—the **income statement**. While a balance sheet is a snapshot at a particular moment, an income statement is a measure of the financial activity of your company over a period, beginning and ending at particular moments, called a fiscal or financial year. The financial year of most small businesses mirrors the calendar year. The balance sheet, then, will be as of December 31, while the income statement will be for the twelve months ending on December 31. The balance sheet shows where the company is. The income statement shows how it got there.

Line one on the income statement is *revenue*—how much product the company sold during the fiscal year. Next, will be the number representing the *cost of goods sold*. Cost of goods sold is, guess what? The direct cost of creating the product, like labor, materials, supplies and direct overhead. Subtract cost of goods sold from revenues and you have the *gross profit*. Gross profit is the profit made on your product before you deduct the costs of selling the product and managing the company.

Selling expense appears next—advertising, sales salaries, commissions and so on.

Next you'll find *general and administrative expenses*. These are the costs of running the back of the house—office salary, your salary, office rent, telephone expenses and so forth.

Just below general and administrative expenses is a category called *other income and expense*. It includes things like interest income and interest expense. Maybe you have company money in a money market account, earning interest until it's needed. The interest earned has nothing to do with your normal business operations and needs to be isolated to avoid confusion. If it were lumped with revenues, it would make sales look bigger than they actually are. Likewise, with non-normal business expenses. You need to isolate them so as not to distort cost of goods sold or sales and general and administrative expenses.

Next step on the income statement is to add together selling, general and administrative expenses, and other income and expenses, and subtract them from gross profit to arrive at *net income before taxes*.

Now, calculate your taxes owed (if you're lucky) on the net income before taxes, subtract what you owe from net income before taxes and you arrive at the final income statement figure—*net income*. Hurrah! May it always be positive.

Statement of Cash Flow

OPENING CASH BALANCE

CASH RECEIVED FROM:
    Cash Sales
    Collection of Accounts Receivable
    Borrowed Money
    Lottery Winnings
        TOTAL CASH RECEIVED
        TOTAL CASH AVAILABLE

CASH SPENT ON:
    Paying Company Expenses
    Paying Company Debt
    Buying Fixed Assets
        TOTAL CASH SPENT

ENDING CASH BALANCE

Finally, there's the *statement of cash flow*. It begins with *cash on hand* at the beginning of the year and ends with cash on hand at the end of the year. It provides the answer you really wanted: Where did all my money go? Sometimes accountants don't prepare this statement for small businesses. Make sure you request one.

All of the figures on your financial statements were drawn directly from your books of original entry (the journals) that you diligently maintained all year long. The balance sheet, income statement and statement of cash flow, then, are simply the end of the process.

I mentioned generally accepted accounting principles earlier. The adherence to GAAP is of fundamental importance in presenting meaningful financial statements. But you need to consider another important aspect when preparing financial statements. You face two methods of business accounting—the cash basis and the accrual basis; one reflects reality, the other is simpler but can be misleading.

Cash basis accounting says a transaction is recorded in the appropriate journal only when cash actually changes hands. That is, when cash physically comes into or goes out of the business. Under cash basis accounting, a sale is recorded only when cash is received for the sale, not when the sale is made. Likewise an expense is recorded only when it's actually paid for, not when it's incurred.

Accrual basis accounting, on the other hand, calls for a transaction to be recorded in the appropriate journal when the transaction takes place, even if cash won't be received or be paid out until some time later. Under accrual basis accounting, a sale made today is recorded today even though the customer may have thirty days to pay for the purchase.

Cash basis accounting makes intuitive sense to many business people because it accurately reflects what happens in their bank accounts. After all, they can't spend the money until they get it and until they pay out the money, they still have it. But of the two accounting methods, the accrual basis is the more valid—the only valid method, in fact—because it provides a truer picture of where a business actually stands financially.

Consider: If I buy something and have thirty days to pay for it, under cash basis accounting the purchase is not acknowledged anywhere in my books or on my financial statements until I actually send the check. I could have many dollars in liabilities and my books and financial statements wouldn't reveal that fact because the transactions are not recorded until I actually pay the liability. The inaccuracy of the cash basis works in reverse for sales. I may have many dollars of sales, as yet unpaid for, that wouldn't show up anywhere until the customers actually pay for them. With cash basis accounting, there's no knowing where the company truly stands financially.

Under accrual basis accounting, in which a transaction is appropriately recorded when it's initially transacted, my books and financial statements reflect a truer financial picture of the business, whether the transaction is a sale or a purchase.

Nobody who understands cash and accrual basis accounting methods would or should accept cash basis books or financial statements to decide anything about a business because cash basis accounting hides as much as it reveals.

The importance of the statement of cash flow is that it bridges the gap between your understanding of your business from a "money in the bank" perspective, while allowing the books to be maintained in the most accurate manner

Financial statements are for you *and* for the outside world. They need to be honest windows into your business. Investors, money lenders and others need to be confident in what the statements are telling them. And in planning for your future, it never hurts to understand your own reality.

By the way, bluffing is for poker, not for conversations about financial statements. Bankers, accountants and anyone else who knows financial statements can spot a bluffer a mile away. Too many business people try to impress others with their knowledge about financial statements when they actually don't know what they're talking about. Financial statement jargon is like a foreign language and those of us who speak it can spot a phony in a minute.

**Would you ever try to bluff a Frenchman
with your high school French?**

Commandment IX: Thou Shalt Be Tax Wise

Know the tax laws regarding your particular business. Be well informed regarding all available deductions and tax advantages.

Death and taxes may be two of life's more unpleasant certainties. While people don't waste their breath complaining about death, hot air and taxes go hand in hand. The grousing and grumbling are unceasing. In all my years in business, I've never met anyone who doesn't pay too much in taxes or, more accurately, *waaay* too much in taxes! They need to get over it.

Like electricity and payroll, taxes are just another cost of doing business. Their appearance on an income statement should not cause wailing and gnashing of teeth. Too many business people, though, are driven to distraction by taxes. Don't put taxes in the driver's seat.

Decisions based solely on tax-annoyance are bad business decisions. Act on sound business principles, period. Giving taxes—or any other individual business expense—the power of veto succeeds only in cramping your creative style. Consider first what's best for the business, and then see if you can make the finances work.

If you're mulling over where to put a new branch office, begin with an unencumbered determination of which location best fits the company's needs. Then run the decision through the appropriate filters, of which the cost of taxes is but one. If the location is wrong for the business, a lower tax bill will not make it right.

The tax system was in place long before you showed up, and it will be there long after you've left the scene. Don't waste effort and energy fighting it. Work to understand the system, make it less intimidating, less frightening. Doing so will help you avoid the sense of panic concerning all things taxes.

In this chapter, we'll review business taxes. We'll examine the tax system itself, where you fit into it and the cost of doing it wrong.

UNDERSTANDING THE SYSTEM

It only seems like you're surrounded. Every time you turn around you seem to be getting a tax bill from some direction. In fact, from top to bottom, only six or so entities have the haunting authority of taxation. Each is an elected body. They are the federal government, state governments, county governments, city governments, any other elected governments and, finally, the board of trustees of your subdivision. That's right, your subdivision fee is really a tax levied by an elected body—the board of trustees.

INCOME TAXES

TAXING AUTHORITY	BASED ON
Federal	Net Corporate Income or Net S Corporation Income (passed thru) or Net Partnership Income (passed thru) or Net Sole Proprietor Income (it's all yours)
State	Same as Federal with minor modifications
Local	Local Income Taxes are rare but some counties/cities have one

The federal government levies taxes on income, payroll and certain industries whose lobbyists couldn't avoid having them taxed.

Most state governments also levy taxes on income and payroll. A few, though, have no state corporate or personal income tax. Those states have other types of taxes, however, to keep treasuries fed. States also tax your company's very existence in the form of an annual corporate registration and/or franchise fee. State governments also levy sales taxes.

PAYROLL TAXES

TAXING AUTHORITY	TYPE	BASED ON
Federal	Withholding Unemployment	Taxes withheld plus Social Security match First $7,000 of employee earnings
State	Withholding Unemployment	Taxes withheld Maximum wage base set by each State
Local		Very rare, but some municipalities have them

County governments can levy property taxes and sales taxes. Likewise, with municipal governments. The sales taxes for both are collected by the state and remitted to the taxing authority based on a formula derived through political debate.

In the any-other-elected-body category, taxes are levied wherever authority is present. Always check with your accountant to see if you are lucky enough to be in an area subject to some special tax.

SALES TAXES

TAXING AUTHORITY	BASED ON
Federal	Sales of specified items. Most businesses are not subject
State	Taxes collected from customers Value of goods brought into the state upon which you would have been liable for tax had they been purchased in your home state
Local	Municipality tax added on to state rate

But that's it. That's a complete list of taxing authorities and the taxes they levy. Not really so frightening, is it? Now let's see how they go about collecting those taxes.

Federal and state governments have the legal authority to appoint you as their agent, to collect taxes for them. These include payroll taxes and sales taxes. As their agent, you are required to collect and remit those taxes in the manner they want them remitted. You don't have a choice. You must deduct payroll taxes from your employees' pay and remit the taxes you withhold by a specific date in a specific manner to the appropriate government agencies.

In the case of the federal government, taxes are remitted through the federal banking system. Any Federal Reserve bank must by law accept remittances and act as a conduit to the federal government. In keeping with the times, it's all done online through a system labeled EFTPS—Electronic Federal Tax Payment System. (It wouldn't be government without an acronym, now would it?) Except for the smallest of businesses, you're required to use EFTPS. The smallest of businesses can file its taxes by filling out a deposit coupon, going to the bank and depositing the coupon and money. Your accountant can explain how it's done.

The deadline to remit payroll taxes varies according to the amount of taxes collected. It extends from as little as within three days of their deduction from an employee's pay to the fifteenth day of the month following the month they are collected from employees. The less frequently you remit the taxes, the bigger the amount you will have to remit. Don't hold on to the government's money for too long. You might spend it on something else.

Remittance is on the honor system, which is all very nice unless you make a mistake, intentionally or otherwise, and get behind. The feds frown on delinquency. Do yourself a favor and get professional help with payroll.

Handling payroll is a complicated task—too complicated and dangerous for novices to play with. Play it smart and use one of the payroll services. They're not expensive and they'll keep you from the edge of a precipitous pitfall. Payroll services "impound" the taxes due, i.e. they escrow your payroll taxes at the same time they pay your employees. They pay your payroll and remit the taxes simultaneously. They then debit your account for the total amount. No muss, no fuss, no mess-ups.

State taxes are usually paid through the use of a payment coupon book. The coupon book contains twelve monthly coupons, similar to mortgage or car payment coupons. Some states require online filing, similar to EFTPS, for larger taxpayers. But most states still accept coupon payment. If the taxes are small enough, they may be paid quarterly or annually. Another question for your accountant!

All other taxes are paid along with the appropriate tax return on some regular schedule.

BECOMING INTIMATE WITH YOUR LIABILITIES

Every business must show the federal government an annual income and expense statement—no exceptions. How that's done, though, depends on the company's organizational structure.

As we discussed in Chapter 1, S corporations and most LLCs, partnerships and sole proprietorships are "pass-through" entities and don't pay taxes themselves. Entity income "passes through" to the owner's personal returns. Regardless, each entity is required to file a federal tax return that shows how much income will "pass through" and to whom. Form K-1 is issued by pass-through entities (except sole proprietorships) showing the Social Security number of the person to whom the income passes, and how much income should be reported.

Sole proprietorships are also "pass-through" organizations and, lacking a K-1, their entire income or loss is reported on a Schedule C that is a part of its owner's personal return.

States follow the feds, having structured their tax laws around the federal return. Whatever federal tax return companies file, there's a state return usually with the same number, which is essentially a summary of the federal return. States get detailed information about a company's income and expenses from a copy of the company's federal return, which is attached to the state return.

Only rarely do companies file more than a federal and state return.

Any business with employees must file Form 941, the federal quarterly payroll tax return. It's due at the end of the month following the end of the quarter. The quarterly payroll return is the government's first inkling of how much in payroll taxes you actually owe for the most recent quarter. These returns show total payroll for the quarter, the taxes you withheld and the amount you deposited, through EFTPS or coupon, to cover those taxes. Ideally, the amounts reported withheld and the amount deposited will be identical.

Companies need to file an annual federal payroll tax return to report the federal unemployment insurance tax. The tax is a tiny, per-employee tax, probably the smallest tax you will ever pay. The money is used to back up state unemployment systems that run short.

Most states have a monthly payroll tax and a monthly sales tax return (Form 940). The due dates are slightly weird: Taxes collected during the first two months of any calendar quarter are usually due on the 15th (withholding) or the 20th (sales) of the month following when the taxes were collected. Taxes collected in the third month of the calendar quarter are not due until the *last* day of the month following the month when the taxes were collected. Go figure. You usually pay the tax with a coupon, sending a check along with it. Check with your accountant for your state's requirements.

The state, too, has an unemployment tax return, which is filed quarterly. The tax rate is based on a company's unemployment claims history. It is due at the end of the month following the end of the quarter.

So, at the federal level, you've got quarterly payroll tax returns and an annual unemployment return. At the state level, you have the monthly payroll tax return, the monthly sales tax return and the quarterly unemployment tax return. All things considered, no big deal. But now you know why there are accountants and why you should not try to do it yourself!

Every business is subject to an obscure tax known as the "use" tax. It's a tax owed on goods bought out of state, brought into the state and upon which no sales taxes were paid. The state government expects to collect the equivalent of sales taxes on those goods. You're supposed to keep track of the value of the out-of-state goods purchased and remit the taxes owed by voluntarily filing a use tax return. Getting caught not paying the tax can be extremely expensive to remedy. Speak with your accountant about how to handle the use tax.

The Internet, with its worldwide reach, has exponentially increased violations of the use tax. When you hear of states fighting to collect taxes on Internet purchases, the taxes being talked about are use taxes. As the volume of Internet purchases increases, and local sales tax revenues decrease, you can bet the states will eventually win in some way.

Some people are under the misimpression that businesses do not have to pay sales taxes on the things they buy. This is only partially true. Sales taxes are always paid by the "ultimate consumer", that is the individual or entity who is last in the chain of ownership of the goods. If a business buys something for resale, in other words it buys something to sell to its customers, and will charge sales tax when the sale takes place, then the business does not have to pay sales tax when the goods are purchased. If a business buys something for its own consumption, then the business is the ultimate consumer and has to pay sales tax when the goods are purchased. Check with your accountant before you decide what you should and should not pay sales taxes on; this can be a complicated issue. So if, and only if, your company is not the final consumer of something, is it exempt from the sales tax on it. If you buy something to resell to your customers, you do not have to pay the tax on it. But if you don't pay the sales tax yourself, you have to collect the tax from your customer and remit it to the state. Either way, you are involved with sales tax, either as payer or collector.

I've mentioned your accountant a lot but remember, *you're* responsible for paying your taxes—not your accountant. You need to keep up and make sure you're getting the appropriate tax forms to sign at the appropriate time.

KNOWING WHAT HAPPENS IF YOU DO IT WRONG

If, for whatever reason, you're unable to pay taxes due, don't compound the problem by not filing the appropriate return. You won't slip by unnoticed. The IRS knows who owes. The state knows who owes. Big Brother is truly watching. You'll simply create a double whammy for yourself. You face penalties for failing to pay taxes and penalties for failing to file the tax returns. Failing to file is the more egregious sin.

Filing a return, even though you can't pay the taxes due, is both an acknowledgment of your responsibility as a taxpayer to file a return, and a confirmation that you owe the taxes. The government is not horrible about late payment. You will pay a penalty for failing to pay on time, but the government will work with you to fashion a reasonable schedule of payments.

Failing to file, on the other hand, is considered tax evasion and that gets the government in an ugly mood. If you don't file, the government must assume that you didn't care to abide by the rules, not that you didn't have the money. What would you think?

In the case of income taxes, you can get an extension to file a return. But you never get an extension to pay. Extensions to file other types of returns are usually not available. With income taxes and payroll taxes, you're supposed to pay in advance of filing a return anyway, so there's no sense asking for an extension if your only reason for being late is that you don't have the money.

If you are a corporation or an LLC, taxes are a liability of the corporation, not of you personally. The corporate veil holds, shielding the individual from personal liability for the taxes.

Liability for payroll taxes withheld from employee wages is a different story. *There is no corporate veil protection for payroll taxes withheld from employees' pay.* These are called the "trust fund" portion of the payroll taxes you owe. If you don't pay them, you're *personally liable* for them, regardless of the corporate structure. The penalty for failing to pay withheld payroll taxes is 100 percent of the unpaid taxes! You are personally liable for double the amount of taxes you did not remit. Don't dabble with payroll taxes. Things can get nasty quickly. Don't dabble with *any* taxes you collect as an agent of the government. The government's very selfish about the money you collect on its behalf.

When it comes to taxes, know what you owe and when you owe it. Even if you can't pay, stay within the rules and the government will treat you reasonably. If the government writes you a letter, don't be rude. Answer it. It is in your best interest to tell the truth on a timely basis. But NEVER try to deal with the taxing authorities yourself. ALWAYS use an accountant. He or she knows the language. Still, the onus is always on your back. Understand the system. Don't fret over it; it's not worth it. Get the help you need and get your taxes filed on time. Taxes need not be the burden they're made out to be.

Look at taxes as a necessary evil. Avoid them when you can, but never evade them. Do you want to live always looking over your shoulder for the tax man?

Commandment X: Thou Shalt Be High Tech

Technology can be your best friend or your worst enemy, depending on your knowledge and technological proficiency.

Just a few years ago, it was said that new integrated processors, the tiny chips that run PCs, doubled in power and halved in size every six months. Electronic evolution at hyper-speed. Amazingly, at the same time, the price of those processors was plummeting. The family-room computer had more computing power than the room-sized computers of the largest corporations a generation before. Bigger, faster, cheaper—a stunning and wonderful confluence of technology and economics.

Meanwhile, software creators are busy fashioning programs and games to harness all that power. Onward and upward we go. It's dizzying.

In this chapter, we'll look at high technology and your business. I realize I'll be preaching to the choir, by and large. If you're thirty-five or younger, computers and the Internet are pretty much facts of life. But I believe the power and possibilities they bring to the world of small business are worth reiterating. So I will.

To those of us old enough to remember a world without megabytes and e-mail, the transformation computers have wrought is pure science fiction. It's no less astounding than it would have been to climb down from your horse and step into a jet. I hope everyone reading this has a chance sometime to know that feeling. It's wonderful, if a tad disorienting.

BUYING ONLY WHAT YOU NEED

It's easy to forget, but a business computer is just another business tool. Too many business people, though, don't think that way. While they'll use a truck until it's positively crying for the junkyard, they'll upgrade their computers because … well … a later version has arrived on the scene. Don't get sucked in. Don't pay for power you don't need.

The general business applications most small businesses need don't require all that mind-boggling computing power. They'd likely run just fine on a computer three or more generations behind the latest and greatest versions—if you could even find a computer three or four generations behind. When you consider that a computer just one generation behind the cutting-edge can be had for half the price of a new one, why spend the extra money? It's a computer, not an alter ego.

I run my business on used equipment. It's a generation behind, for sure, but it was a fraction of the cost of new and still has more power than I need. I have so little invested in my workstations that when they become too slow, I give them away and buy replacements. Many companies sell computers that have just come off corporate leases and are in fine shape. Big company information technology (IT) departments are always trying to stay current and big budgets abound, so large organizations are always discarding perfectly good equipment. Their extravagance is our windfall. Find a reliable vendor and spend as little as you have to. If you really want to splurge, get yourself a brand new laptop or a big-screen monitor as a special treat. Watch the specials. Don't pay for excessive power or storage and match your level of sophistication with your computer's. No sense buying a turbo V-8 when a reliable V-6 will do!

From the moment you hire your first employee, you'll want to be able to network computers. So make sure the computer you buy is network-ready. Adding networking capability to a non-networked computer can be expensive—more expensive than buying network-ready equipment in the first place. And, if all goes according to plan, you'll be needing to network soon.

A word to the wise: Be careful of trying to build your system yourself. You may think you're computer-savvy, but if you make the wrong buy, correcting the mistake can be costly. Get help. Find a consultant, tell him or her what you're doing, that price is a concern, and listen. If he tries to sell you on a bucketful of bells and whistles, get a second opinion. You don't need bells and whistles. Walk before you try to run.

With software programs such as *Peachtree* and *Microsoft Office*, you could run General Electric. Imagine what they can do for your small business. It's almost impossible to buy software that's not more than what a small business needs. And as your business grows, the software will be well up to the task. *Peachtree* and *Microsoft Office* are not the only quality programs. Look around and ask questions. But remember, business software is just like golf clubs: People who can't use them well are always looking for something new to improve their game. I've always believed that Arnold Palmer could outplay me with a broomstick used properly. If you can't run your business with *Peachtree* and *Microsoft Office,* don't blame the software.

Learn the programs you buy, even if that means taking a course or two. Don't be intimidated; today's software is truly user-friendly. You will actually learn things about business management and record keeping from the software itself. It will automatically ask you to do things you may never have heard of. Know how to navigate with your own software, even though you may not be the software point-person in the company.

Don't rely on a secretary or your mother-in-law to know everything about how your system runs. You should know it, too. One great benefit of financial software is its ability to rearrange information in moments into all manner of analytical tools. A couple of keystrokes or mouse clicks can reveal eye-opening angles on where your company stands. You'll only uncover such helpful information by exploring the software on your own.

SURFING THE NET

Netwise, be there or be square.

From a business standpoint, the Net is the greatest thing since electronic calculators. Your business is as good as the next guy's, no matter how small you are or how big he is. The Net is the great equalizer. Use it to the max.

A computer, a phone line and a dash of DSL, the most common high-speed Web connection, are all you need. Add a Web

site—your electronic business card, brochure and salesman—
and a world full of customers gains access to your store and
products 24/7/365.

While you're snuggled in bed, your Web site will be working. Not having a Web site is like telling the world you don't
want to talk or do business. Just a page or two will do,
announcing your company and its wares.

Create your site yourself or find a Web site developer.
Unless you have all kinds of time and enjoy dabbling, you're
probably better off letting someone do it for you. Developers
are plentiful and they're not terribly expensive.

Make the site interactive if you can afford it. Interactivity
can help you strike while the iron's hot, allowing customers to
find and order your products in one smooth motion. One true
benefit of Internet selling is that it takes advantage of impulse
buying. As soon as you make your customers wait until
tomorrow morning to contact you, you've mainstreamed them
into normal buying habits. Try to reel them in while they're
hot for your product. Short of interactivity, a prominent e-mail
address or a phone number will let customers contact you and
start a dialogue. Your Web site is a portal to sales from all corners of the Earth. Do what you can, the very best you can, at
the price you can afford. But one way or the other, do it.

E-mail is flexible, fast and free. It lets you communicate
with customers anywhere in the world—instantly and en
masse. You can negotiate with them, make them aware of new
offers, introduce new products, or just pass on items of interest, unobtrusively and inexpensively.

E-mail is also an ideal way to communicate with vendors.
You can place orders and track them on their way to your
store, find out about special deals and get questions answered
about product specs—without being put on hold.

Amazon.com, eBay, and shopping sites of their ilk, are customer magnets. The number of daily visitors to such sites is astounding. Shoppers by the millions look for products and are ready to buy. They don't care who you are or where you are. If you've got what they want at the right price, they'll buy from you.

You spend money left and right on advertising, trying to bring customers through the door and making the phone ring. Amazon, eBay and the others are cheap by comparison, and reach a whole new customer base—from Paris to Peoria, and all points in-between. The sites never complain, never sleep and work cheap. They're role-model salesmen as far as I'm concerned.

Shopping sites are also handy market research tools. From the privacy of your office you can browse the competition, see what they're doing and how they're doing it. Or search for new vendors. Whatever. Explore. Be creative. The possibilities are endless.

Best of all, on the Web you can run with the big dogs. The Internet neutralizes the natural advantage of bigness, such as resources and reach. The playing field is leveled and everybody has a chance to win, big guy and little guy alike.

But I'll bet it won't be that way forever. In my darker moments, I'm haunted by visions of the big guys finally figuring out ways to flex their muscles in cyberspace. A time may come when they'll elbow their way to the front and reassert their dominance in the field. Maybe not, but history suggests otherwise. For now, they haven't fully figured out how to get their arms around the Net, but you know they're trying hard. So, take advantage of the window of opportunity while it's open. It might not be open for long.

PROTECTING YOURSELF

Newton's Third Law tells us, "For every action, there's an equal and opposite reaction." For all the wonder computers and the Internet have brought to our world, they've brought vulnerability, too. The Internet door swings both ways. While it lets you out into the world, it can likewise let others in. Be apprehensive and protect yourself.

Sick, geeky nuts make it their sole goal to wreak havoc on computers worldwide—just because they can. Taking advantage of vulnerabilities in operating systems, they create viruses designed to infect computers and harm them and the information they hold. From the start, set your computer to automatically update your operating system with the latest security patches. Buy and install a quality antivirus program that updates virus protections daily. Security updates are free and antivirus programs are inexpensive. Some small-business programs are free, offered by your Internet service provider (ISP) or by the antivirus software companies themselves. ISPs have a vested interest in keeping the Internet clean. By preventing you from picking up viruses, they prevent you from spreading them inadvertently. Don't get caught with your firewall down.

Internet access is wonderful, but it's also not secure. If you take payments from customers over the Net, subscribe to a secure service that will protect the transaction from hackers. Over-protect yourself. A byte of protection is worth a gigabyte of cure.

Backing up your system is another absolute must. Computers can go down and take everything they hold with them. If your computer crashes and you're appropriately backed up, you've faced an aggravation, but little more. If you're not properly backed up, a crash is devastating—the agony of delete. Get help from a qualified consultant. Back up your system often and right. The only thing worse than not being properly backed up is thinking you are and finding too late that you weren't. And don't be afraid of paper. Make plenty of "hard copies."

The concept of a "paperless society" was a figment of someone's imagination. Paper is inexpensive and abundant. Never fail to save something because it was a "waste of paper." And buy decent paper. One of the only permanent contacts you have with your customers is through printed matter. Dingy paper is dingy. Buy bright paper (90 bright or higher) and make everyone feel subconsciously better.

Don't save money on protecting your system. Don't waste it either. Most importantly, be sure it's done right.

KNOWING WHEN TO UPGRADE

"If it ain't broke, don't fix it" rings true even in the age of high tech. If your system is doing the job just fine, don't be tempted to make it better.

A computer is like a car. As long as it's getting you where you want to go, it doesn't need replacing. You may want the newer model, but you don't "need" it. If you're a techie and you just like to be on the leading edge, OK. But don't kid yourself. It has nothing to do with your business. As far as the business is concerned, the fewer upgrades you make the better.

Upgrading costs go beyond just the cost of the machines, which admittedly have been falling. Peripheral costs, both out-of-pocket and operational, can add up quickly. Your software may not be up to a new machine's specifications, meaning you may need to buy new software. Business software is a great buy, but it's not petty cash cheap. You also have no guarantee your old files will be compatible with the new software. And new software often requires retraining for your employees. That's an error-prone, work-slowing, learning-curved, demoralizing hassle to be sure. For no real gain either. "New and improved" software versions are often barely even marginally better than the old, with their "new features" focused on functions you may not even need. What the software makers really did was to rework the software's programming to harness the power of the new machines. It's a game software and hardware manufacturers play to get us to "upgrade." In the automobile industry, it's called "planned obsolescence." Trying to keep up is like betting against the house at a casino—you won't win. Refuse to play. If it's doing the job, your computer is state-of-the-art.

Upgrade when the computer's no longer up to it—when the foot-through-the-screen meter is peaking in the "red-danger" sector. Or upgrade when a new program you need for the business is too advanced for your system. You'll know when to upgrade. It will be obvious.

Frequent upgrading fosters inconsistency and that's exactly the wrong signal to send. Remember, bankers like boring. They like same ol', same ol'. You should, too. Bells and whistles and mighty-megahertzed machines may be fun and ego satisfying, but they have nothing to do with good business practice.

Information technology is the one area where all businesses can be created equal. Why be a minor league player when you can be a pro?

Commandment XI: Thou Shalt Be Properly Insured

Protect yourself, your business and your future.

Insurance is nothing but a nod to Murphy's Law. If something bad can happen, it will. So we insure against it—whatever "it" might be. The very idea has always bugged me.

Insurance is too much like betting against yourself. You pay and pay and pay and the only way to win is to lose. You must have some mighty calamity come crashing down upon you in order to "win." Life insurance is worst of all. Sure a payout will eventually be made—but not to you. To me, that's taking the idea of winning entirely too far.

Of course, these are the ravings of my emotional, irrational side. Intellectually, I know insurance is the prudent choice. Fact is, I am properly insured and proud of it. The only thing worse than betting against myself is the thought of exposing everything I've worked for to the vagaries of life and a litigious society.

In this chapter, we'll look at the world of business insurance. We'll review the types of insurance you need to know about, and we'll talk about getting help and doing it right. Finally, we'll discuss costs and strategies to cover them.

Sometimes, I think the best insurance salespeople in the world are mothers. They teach us to fear impending doom and to protect ourselves from getting hurt. That's why we buy insurance. Too bad moms don't get commissions.

UNDERSTANDING INSURANCE PRODUCTS

Insurance in business is as inevitable as paying taxes and keeping records. Unlike taxes and records, though, insurance is rife with pitfalls. It is expensive, full of fine print and exceptions, and is normally expressed in barely decipherable language.

Fundamentally, business insurance falls into three categories: property and casualty, life and health, and workers' compensation.

Property and Casualty

General Liability	Building and Contents Accidents Non-owned Vehicle
Product Liability	*Most* damages
Special Policies	Errors & Omissions Personal Umbrella Performance Bonds

Property and casualty insurance protects business assets and your personal investment in the business. It, too, falls into three categories: general liability, product liability and special policies.

General liability insurance in business is much like the insurance you carry on your house. It covers your building and its contents from fire, theft, whatever. It also covers people who get hurt on your property, or who are hurt by an employee in the course of business. And it covers vehicles, particularly non-company-owned vehicles used in the business. If an employee has an accident while using his car to take deposits to the bank, your non-owned-vehicle coverage covers such costs as medical bills and repairs. Even more importantly, if you should get sued, the insurance covers legal fees, which can be greater than the claim itself.

Likewise with *product liability insurance*. If your product is a component in someone else's product, and the other person's product injures someone, you may be sued. It's the "machine gun" approach—sue everyone in sight who may in any way be remotely connected and hope somebody has some money, and is deemed to be at fault and will have to pay a claim. You can imagine how expensive that can become.

Special property and casualty insurance includes policies for *errors and omissions, personal liability umbrella* insurance and *special risk* policies.

Performance bonding is a particularly cumbersome issue for small businesses. By issuing a performance bond, the insurance company guarantees the owner of a project that the bonded subcontractor (your company) will complete its work on time.

In construction, one guy's work often begins when the other guy's work stops. This natural dovetailing of work is extremely important in the pace of completion of the total project. Missed schedules can increase costs considerably.

Project managers want to be protected against the failure of individual contractors to perform according to contract. Thus, performance bonds.

Sadly, performance bonding of new companies comes with a classic "Catch 22." Without a company having a track record of completing work on time, insurance companies generally won't bond the new company. That cuts new companies out of a lot of projects, making it hard to establish a track record.

Life and Health

Group Plans	Medical & Dental Life Prescriptions
Key Man	What would you do without him?
Buy/Sell	How well do you like your partner's spouse?

Life and health insurance are generally sold on a group basis and are used as employee benefits. Most of us are at least somewhat familiar with these policies because we're likely to have been covered by them at some point. As an employer buying these types of insurance for your employees, you suddenly become the "administrator" of the group policies.

When shopping for group insurance, you want to strike a balance between the benefits you wish to offer and their costs. You'll need to explore the components of group insurance, including medical, dental, vision and prescription drug coverage. What will you offer? What deductibles and co-pays will your group face?

Nothing says you have to pay any part of the policy's costs. Your employees can carry the whole freight. Simply making a group health plan available to your employees is in itself a plus.

As administrator, you'll also be required to keep the insurance company informed of the makeup of your covered workforce—ages, positions, compensation and so forth. The insurance company will want to be updated each month. That's one more thing to take care of, but you can do it—with proper help. Have your agent by your side when you're learning to manage a group plan.

Should you consider "self-insurance?" When you self-insure, you play the odds the insurance company plays. You buy a policy with a high deductible and commit your company to cover some or all deductible costs. As with high-deductible collision insurance, high-deductible health insurance is substantially cheaper. You're gambling that the money you save on the high-deductible policy premium will be greater than the total of the deductibles you have to pay.

On paper, self-insurance can seem like an excellent way to keep down costs. But it's not a small-business game. Self-insurance can be tricky and, as a rule, requires deep pockets. In the blink of an eye, this "cost saver" can become an expensive black hole. Don't risk it. It's out of your league.

Key man insurance protects a business from the cost of hiring a replacement for a "key man or woman" who dies. Generally, the "key man or woman" is a stock-holding partner. Replacing a partner, particularly a founding partner, may require the hiring of one or even two employees at substantial salaries. If the business partners had been taking small salaries topped off with year-end bonuses based on company results, the addition of a substantial salary or two could be devastating to the business. Key man insurance covers those additional costs.

Buy/sell insurance is another form of key man insurance. It's based on a legally drawn buy/sell agreement that prevents a shareholder in a closely held company from selling his stock to anyone other than the parties stipulated in the agreement. The agreement is designed to protect the partners from being forced to accept a new partner not of their choosing.

The buy/sell agreement comes into play if a partner dies and his or her stock in the company becomes part of his or her estate. The estate is required by the buy/sell agreement to sell the stock to the company at a pre-arranged price. By insuring the life of each partner in the amount of the cost of buying their stock from their estates, the buy/sell insurance guarantees the company will have the money to buy the stock.

Workers' compensation insurance covers your employees' ability to earn a living and pay medical bills if they're hurt or incapacitated while on the job. Workers' comp is mandated by the state and closely regulated by your state insurance department. Its premiums are set by the state and can be expensive.

The premiums are determined according to state-defined employee risk factor categories. The risk of injury to construction workers, for instance, is considered greater than that of retail workers, and they would fall into separate categories. Be certain your employees are properly categorized. A mistaken categorization might mean paying higher premiums than necessary. You absolutely need the advice of an insurance agent to properly address this issue.

In some states, a minimum number of employees must be reached before workers' compensation insurance is required. Ignore the minimum. Have the insurance from your first employee forward. The cost of not having the insurance when an injury occurs is mind-boggling, particularly if negligence was involved. You can be held personally liable, corporate veil or no. Don't risk it. And make safety on the job, job one.

On-the-job injuries are not only expensive; they're disruptive to your operation. Create an effective safety program and follow through. Include first aid training and CPR courses. Be actively involved. Your employees will follow your lead. If you demonstrate seriousness about the program and a commitment to safety on the job, they will too. Safety doesn't cost, it pays.

LISTENING TO THE EXPERTS

With insurance, the devil truly is in the details. Listening to an agent describe and compare insurance can be mind-numbing. That's why we need them. Your insurance agent should play as big a role in your business as any other adviser. If your agent won't, you need a different agent.

Selecting coverage that is a perfect fit for your business is an important first step. Your agent needs to study the subtleties of your business' activities and determine where you may be exposed. Insurance that leaves gaps in areas where claims are likely to happen isn't much good.

Ideally, work with an agent with experience in your field. Industry specialization is not unusual in the insurance business. To find an agent with specific industry background, look through trade publications or ask your trade associations.

Finally, understand the coverage you have. Thinking you're covered for something, only to find out you're not, can be disastrous. Be curious and quiz your agent. Better yet, have the agent interpret your policies for you.

PAYING ATTENTION TO COSTS

That insurance is expensive is a given. Let's look at how those expensive premiums are calculated.

Property and casualty insurance premiums generally are calculated on one of three factors: the size of your payroll, the amount of your gross revenue, or the value of your property.

Estimated payroll is an indication of the number of people you employ in your business. The more employees, the more likely you are to have accident claims. Other factors also matter: the kind of work being done and how much your employees are paid, for instance. Injuries are far more likely if you have a factory employing a lot of low-wage laborers, than if you employ a few highly paid executives or professionals. It's the nature of the work each group does. In assessing risk, which determines the premiums, underwriters use gross payroll to tell them a lot about your organization.

Estimated revenue, another measuring stick, indicates the size and complexity of the company. A $1 billion company will obviously be more complicated than a $100,000 company, and insurance rates will reflect that.

Property values pretty much speak for themselves. This approach is most familiar because it's the same one we experience in our personal insurance. The value of your buildings, their contents, including inventory values, will factor directly into the size of your premium.

A fundamental difference between personal insurance and business insurance is the calculation of premiums. With personal insurance, the situation or property being covered is not likely to change during the term of the policy. You pay a premium based on the risk when the policy was issued. But in business, situations and circumstances change constantly. Employees come and go, property is bought and sold, inventory levels fluctuate and so on. Business insurance premiums, therefore, are *estimated* when the policy is issued. Then, when the policy terminates, the insurance company does an audit to determine what actually happened during the policy's term and adjusts the estimated premium to an actual premium. It may go up or down. You either get a bill or a refund, depending on what the audit revealed.

Underestimating your payroll or revenue to get a lower up-front premium is a fool's game. The audit, which is done soon after the policy term expires, will reveal the underestimation and you'll get a whopping adjustment-to-actual bill and your next year's premium, also based on the audit, will be much higher.

Be aware, some insurance policies carry minimum premiums. The insurance company demands a minimum level of premium to make the coverage profitable. So, a small business with its small risks is often subject to the minimum premium and may end up paying the same insurance premiums slightly bigger companies pay.

Annual insurance premiums can be a huge burden for small businesses. Fortunately, premium financing is available to help to minimize their impact. As with any loan, there is a finance charge and usually a slight service charge, but you can pay the premium periodically over the policy's term. Ask your agent.

Premiums vary widely from company to company. Shopping the market can save you a substantial amount. An independent insurance agent—who represents multiple companies—can shop the market for the best prices, while making sure the coverage offered is equivalent.

Premium shopping, though, can be overdone. Adding new customers is expensive for insurance companies. They want to renew you year after year. If you get the reputation of a constant price shopper, you might find it harder or more expensive to get insurance.

When you buy insurance, you're buying a service. You want the best quality at the best price. But most importantly, you need it to be there when you need it. Price isn't everything.

**Aren't you better off being
safe than sorry?**

Commandment XII: Thou Shalt Balance Thy Life

Balance means maintaining personal relationships, staying healthy and giving yourself a well needed break now and then.

Remember your first exposure to a newborn child of your own? It was probably one of the most awesome experiences you have ever had. You beheld this new life, this creation that you dreamed of for nine months, this scary newcomer with everything you have experienced still to be experienced. The new responsibilities you anticipated are suddenly here and, it occurs to you, irreversible. Can you handle it? Are you up to it? Will you know what to do? Your family has to adjust to this wonderful intruder who will occupy space and time and money and all of your personal resources.

Now replace the words "newborn child" in the first sentence with "new business" and re-read the first paragraph.

The all-consuming nature of a new small business shocks the systems of entrepreneurs and everyone around them. They expect lots of work and long hours. But they're often stunned by the jarring realization of just how far out there they are. Everything is on the line and it's all up to them. The business is heading for warp speed—and they're trying to learn on the job.

In this chapter, we'll talk about the need for keeping life in balance. We'll discuss some strategies for dealing with stress, too.

Your business might overwhelm you, but you can survive with a smile.

IDENTIFYING STRESS

I've got a friend who occasionally puts on a few pounds. Each time he sheds the weight, he solemnly swears he won't regain it. But he always does. What drives him crazy, though, is not the weight gain itself, but that he sees the same pattern play itself out over and over—yet he can't stop it. The same bad habits resurface, triggering the same rationalizations and the same gain of five or ten pounds. And when do the bad habits resurface? When he needs his mental energy for something other than worrying about his diet. When stress and despair make him feel entitled to that doughnut. When nervousness about the future makes him want to make the present more comfortable.

I hope you slimmed down in preparation for your bout with your new business, because you and Krispy Kreme will likely get to know each other very well. High stress levels are part of the daily routine of business owners. For most people, the outward signs of stress are readily identifiable—problems sleeping, short fuse and so on. The tricky part is not rationalizing away those signs. Don't pretend they don't mean what they mean. Don't assume you can "handle it." When you recognize the signs, you need to deal with stress directly and immediately. Untreated stress grows exponentially in its power and ability to grip you. And everyone and everything around you will suffer, including your business. Stress goes hand in hand with lousy decision-making. Control it.

Managing stress should be an everyday part of your behavior, like sleep, diet and exercise. Shelves in bookstores and libraries are loaded with tomes and tapes on managing stress. Pick out a couple and absorb them. Find time for your personal stress-management outlets. Maybe it's walking or napping, a round of golf or reading a good book. Maybe you like to meditate. Or work a Sudoku puzzle (my weakness). All are wonderful, practical options. Vacations are rarely the answer. Worries like to travel, too. You'll be told you need rest, but what you really need is a diversion. Whatever works, though, build it into your schedule. Learn to discharge steam from the boiler before it blows.

Stress comes with the territory of owning a small business. Accept it upfront and learn to live with it. Don't be afraid to be a bit selfish about what you need to keep it together physically and psychologically. The single most important asset you have in the business is you. Protect and nurture that asset because when you're not running on all cylinders, neither is your business.

And remember to smile. Laughter is powerful medicine. Your business is serious business, for sure, but don't take it all too seriously. You work hard, you do your best and you'll live to fight another day. Be glad. Learn to smile at the twists

and turns in the road. A bit of humor can be like the proverbial "spoonful of sugar" that makes the medicine go down, if
not delightfully, at least more easily. And you'll be surprised
at the effect that can have on the people around you. When
the captain can smile and get on with command, the crew
redoubles its efforts. Save your furrowed brow for the really
big stuff.

When everything is a crisis, nothing is a crisis. Crisis mode
just becomes the way you do business—a stomach-souring,
morale-zapping modus operandi. That's a true crisis. Put a
sign on your office wall that wonders, "What difference does
it make?" Read it whenever you're disturbed, or when you
are about to launch an attack on someone or something. As
you cool down, you'll discover most would-be crises aren't
worth the worry. In the big picture, an errant brush stroke or
two rarely makes the difference.

Rudyard Kipling wrote a wonderful poem, "If..." I keep a
copy of it on the wall in my office. Look it up and read it.

BALANCING RISK

Starting a business involves risk. You can't get around that.
When you open the doors, you expose your neck. By definition, a small-business owner is a risk-taker. Don't waste your
time scheming to make safe what is inherently dangerous. It
can't be done. But danger can be managed.

Managing danger is what *The Twelve Commandments for
Small Business* is all about. If you erase all risk, you won't
make any money. No pain, no gain. No risk, no reward. It's
how you manage risk that counts.

What is your risk tolerance?

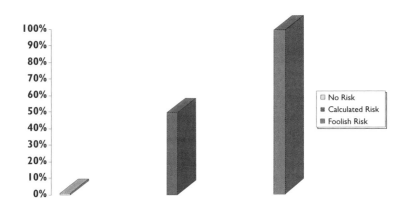

We talked earlier about the spectrum of risk—from no risk to calculated risk to foolish risk. You want to be in the middle, taking calculated risks. That way you clearly know all of the variables and how they interact. You know the predictable outcomes based on those variables and you find all of the outcomes acceptable, win or lose.

Correct assessment of the level of risk of a course of action is critical. In small business, and throughout your life, depend on sounding boards—people whose judgment you trust and who will be honest with you. Bounce your ideas off them and hear what they say. You might not agree or follow their advice, but hear them out. Don't dismiss an unwanted perspective. But don't summarily bow to it either. Weigh it carefully and be open and honest with yourself.

The sobering fact is that starting a business borders on foolish risk. You don't know all the variables, and the outcomes are not all acceptable to you. Slot machines at the local casino are closer to calculated risk than starting a small business. The slots pay out at better than a 90 percent clip, while small businesses fail at greater than a 60 percent clip. If slots only paid out 40 percent of the time, no one would play. It's what this book is about, helping you to learn the variables and turn "foolish" into "calculated."

Speaking of casinos, let's talk about "double or nothing." It doesn't work. Small-business people, though, try it all the time. When things are going down, good money after bad won't turn things around. You might be tempted to believe in magic bullets because the other option is admitting failure. Keep your head about you. Don't make desperate decisions under stress.

INCLUDING YOUR FAMILY

Risk? Stress? I haven't even mentioned what it's like to come home after a bad day and have to deal with a family who would prefer you have a "normal" job, rather than be president of a budding empire.

Remember that you'll have "passengers" along with you on your small-business train. They'll be no more able to disembark than you can if the trip gets rocky. They'll be facing the consequences as surely as you will. If you didn't include your family in your planning when things were new and exciting, how can you expect your family to "be there for you" when the going gets tough? Make your family a part of things from the start. Doing so will make ultimate success better, and failure, should it come, tolerable.

Talk with your spouse and family about what you'd like to do. Be honest with them about the risks and the demands. For a long time, the new business will necessarily come first. Make them aware of that. Ask for their permission and support before you jump in.

If they say no, don't do it. Even a successful small business will be incredibly disruptive to their lives. A failing business will require even more from them. Apologies after the fact won't wash. Business failure and divorce too often go hand in hand.

Your family is your first responsibility and your most treasured asset. Don't make family members your victims. To fail in business is unfortunate. To lose your family is unthinkable.

If the decision is "go for it," your family will be excited and proud. Find ways to include them. Let them share in the challenge. The more they feel a part, the better they'll handle the demands. Understanding breeds understanding and makes every trial easier to bear. Don't fool yourself into thinking that insulating your family from the stresses and strains of the business is somehow heroic. It's impossible to do anyway and will only make them feel isolated and vulnerable.

Whether the outcome is success or failure, life will go on. Success in your family life need not be tied to success in business.

HANDLING SUCCESS AND FAILURE EQUALLY

Success is like currency—it needs to be banked. Remember your successes. Make note of them. Revel in them. Celebrate everything, big and small. Look for mini-victories. Observe anniversaries—week-to-week, month-to-month, year-to-year. The longer you survive, the more likely you'll continue to survive.

And share the spoils. Post customer appreciation letters for all to see. Let your employees know when they do good work. Make them feel part of a team. Show your appreciation in little, thoughtful ways that make them feel special.

Be true to yourself. Do your best and be proud. Appreciating success will help you handle failure if it comes. Handle both with equanimity.

And know when to say when. Believing in yourself and your business does not mean closing your eyes to reality. The signs of a failing enterprise are generally easy to spot. The tough part is opening your eyes to them. The first one to identify when he is losing will always lose the least. That's not to say throw in the towel when the going gets tough. But it does suggest that you closely examine any signs of failure so that you know if they are fatal. Work with your closest advisers on this.

If you move quickly enough, you will leave with energy, grace and dignity. You need not feel ashamed of failure, as long as you know in your heat of hearts that you tried the very best you could.

Make sure you have something left financially, psychologically and physically to come back and fight with to achieve your next success.

Personal reward is easier to obtain than financial reward. Aren't you entitled to a break once in a while?

Commandment XIII: Thou Shalt Deliver Fine Quality

No matter what you do in business you must deliver a fine level of quality. The level of quality you need to deliver is indicative of the market you are reaching out to.

Maybe I worked as a baker in a previous life. That might explain why my dozen commandments actually total thirteen. Or maybe I am just practicing what I preach—giving a little extra. Whatever the explanation, there is a thirteenth commandment included in *The Twelve Commandments for Small Business.* If you can't abide by this bonus commandment, "Thou shalt deliver fine quality," the first twelve won't do you much good.

Delivering quality may seem like a no-brainer. Most people venture into business with a sincere desire to do the world one better. But quality requires a balancing act. Too much or too little and the scale tips; then both outcomes are bad. Both can take your business down.

In this chapter, the last commandment (I promise), we'll look at quality and perception of quality. If what you offer is what customers want, your quality equation is just right. Keeping it that way is your challenge.

OVER-PROMISING, OVER-DELIVERING

With so much competition in the world, what will make someone choose your little business? Your quality.

Quality, service and price are the three focal points of business competition. A generation ago, the mantra was you had to provide two of the three to succeed. If you had a quality product and offered excellent service, you could charge a bit more than your competition and still do fine. Or if you had a quality product and the price was right, you could get by without sterling service. But in a world of commodities, where everyone offers the same products, quality of product is a moot point. Prices can vary, but not wildly, because customers can simply go next door and get the product cheaper. That leaves service as the true difference maker.

There's a certain "been there, done that" appeal to discovering a new product or business. People love to discover a new shop or restaurant and brag to their friends about it. They actually get excited about a new small business opening its doors, much more so than if a corporate giant sends a mailer announcing it's setting up shop in the local mall. People know what *they* have to offer. But they don't know what you've got. Hope springs eternal.

Folks are looking for something special. New businesses—in fact, all smart small businesses—try harder to please than the corporate giants. People get excited about new businesses because they want to experience the difference. It may sound trendy, but focus on "experience." Unlike your larger competitors, you can provide a shopping or service "experience" to your customers. Study Nordstrom, which is the exception. The department store chain concentrates on the entire experience, not just shopping. When you walk in, you get the feeling that you are entering more than just a store. Whether it's the bistro that greets you as you enter, or the grand piano playing, or the way you are served by staff, it is an experience. Zero in on the total experience. What you offer that most big guys can't is a sense of personal connection—a quality connection.

Your business is small and truly on the level of individual customers. You and your employees are not just spokes in some big wheel, you're real people wanting to satisfy me, a customer, who has walked through your door. People sense that and they like it. And that feeling can keep them coming back, because customers know they honestly matter to you.

Learn the art of service and teach it to your employees. A well-trained staff that feels as good about the operation as you do is your key to success, and the key to enhancing customers' perception of the quality they're getting. Of course, your product or service must truly be a quality product or service. But your method of delivery is what sets you apart.

If you'll be serving your customer, you'll have to decide exactly what you will deliver. You may be tempted to ask people what they want and then respond. If you do this, you are putting the responsibility for your product on the wrong shoulders. Your product is *yours* to define. You know more about it than your customer. If you don't, you should not be selling it. The customer is always the customer, but contrary to popular belief, the customer is not always right. To live by the creed "the customer is always right" suggests that when customers complain about something, anything, you should change your business model to accommodate them. That's a mistake. You can't allow customers to determine how you run your business. On the other hand, if you're hearing a complaint consistently, you need to carefully weigh the validity of what's being said and consider making a change.

To maintain quality, you'll want to please your customers as much as you can. But you run your business, not the customer. Customers should be treated with dignity and respect, but you should politely set limits that keep your business on the track you've set. Your company has policies and procedures for a reason, and they shouldn't be abandoned at the first grumblings of a customer. To hand off a difficult situation, your employees should be trained to respond to challenges with a polite, "Let me check with my boss (or the owner) about that." You can then make the call. You may decide to "give in," but that doesn't mean the customer was necessarily right. It simply means you decided to bend a bit in this instance for the long-run good of the business. But be careful. Bending too often voids your policies. If you are tempted to break your own rules often, change the rules.

You also should be aware of the feelings of your employees. If a situation between an employee and a customer flares, don't admonish your employee in front of the customer. A public berating undermines morale, not just of the employee being scolded, but of every other employee. Employees want to know you'll stand behind them. After all, they're only trying to follow the policies and procedures you created.

You need to anticipate your customers' wants and needs and train your people to deal with them. If an employee makes a mistake, a quiet word in your office can put matters right. There's no profit in a spectacle. Good employees are harder to find than customers.

Finally, in addition to the great experience and product you provide, add some icing to the cake. Some restaurants in the food court at the mall always seem to be offering tasty little samples of their products. Likewise, stores like Sam's Club and Costco always offers free samples. You can make a lunch out of them. The ploy undoubtedly works, resulting in sales. I've bought after trying. But a bonus is that it makes those businesses a little bit special in the minds of customers. Follow their lead. Find ways to make doing business with your company a little more special. A small surprise goes a long way. Customers appreciate it and their perception of the quality they get from you will climb. Perception is reality.

UNDERSTANDING QUALITY

Just because you've built a better mousetrap doesn't mean a path will be beaten to your door anytime soon. The mousetrap-buying public is by nature a tough audience. Incremental improvements likely won't win the day, especially if the changes don't capture more mice than the older version. Sometimes, the old traps do just fine. Newer mousetraps on the market tend to be cosmetically more appealing, but will people really spend more for this element of improvement? After all, mousetraps are hidden in dark places, so who will pay the extra buck for a prettier one?

Too much quality can doom your business. People always want the best, but they rarely want to pay for it. Your job is to align the quality of your product with the quality perception of your customers. The flair of imported strawberries on a dinner salad will unquestionably increase your cost, but probably not your customers' willingness to pay more for the salad. The salad isn't worth that much to them, imported strawberries or not.

Avoid the Anguish of QPL

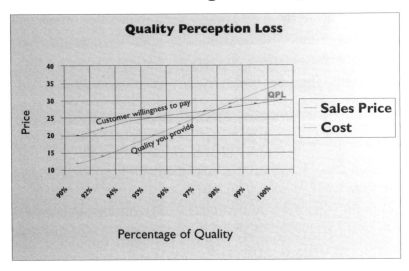

I call this factor QPL—quality perception loss. QPL is the tipping point when quality provided becomes greater than quality perceived. The cost of producing the product exceeds the price customers are willing to pay, so you're losing money. More businesses get ensnared in this trap than you can imagine.

Businesspeople who take great pride in their work are often QPL victims. The carpenter who uses the finest woods and stains to make products targeted to the discount market is a QPL poster boy. What he provides is mismatched with what he can charge. You're in business to make money after all.

Providing perceived quality need not be expensive. The same food served on a white tablecloth is perceived to be better than food served on Formica. An oil change place I frequent vacuums the driver side floor. It takes little effort by the shop but makes me think of its service as a cut above. A nicely laid out shop with a cultured ambiance can have the same quality-suggesting effect on customers. On the other hand, the cluttered, dimly lit antique shop where undiscovered treasures might lurk beneath this or behind that can inspire the thrill of the hunt for the "rare find." This is a quality-enhancing trait in its own right. Music while on hold, or even a sales message, is appreciated. We all hate wondering if we've been disconnected while we're waiting for service.

A great compliment to a small business is when customers assume you are a franchise. Looking like a franchise is a sure sign of quality to customers. Franchises smack of reliability. Successful franchises are by their nature well thought out businesses. They're run by proven formulas and have an extreme customer-comforting effect. McDonald's' reliability has kept the customers coming for years. A McDonald's in Missouri is pretty much like a McDonald's in California or New York or New Zealand. You can count on the consistency of the food and the cleanliness all around. McDonald's is the choice even when better food at a better price might be just across the street, because there's less risk in choosing McDonald's. Understand the depth of the compliment if someone asks if you're a franchise. It is high praise for sure.

Managing the perception of quality is a profitable art form. Credit card companies offer gold and platinum cards because they make people feel special. Not just anybody gets a gold card; you have to be a "preferred" customer. Offering a plain vanilla version of your product makes the one with hot fudge seem better, and the one with hot fudge and nuts seem better still. It's simply a pricing hierarchy. You can charge significantly more without adding much in the way of costs. It's all in the presentation.

People like to fly first class. Offer them a first-class product to step up to. If you don't, you're missing a profitable boat.

CREATING QUALITY CONTROL

Aligning the quality you provide with customers' quality perceptions is half the battle. The other half is keeping the two aligned. Quality control is the key.

Keeping your customers and yourself on the same wavelength requires constant vigilance. Fortunately, you and your customers want to be on the same wavelength—you want them satisfied and they want to be satisfied. To see how you're doing, go straight to the horse's mouth. Ask your customers—constantly.

How did we do today? How did you hear about us? Be sincere with your questions and you'll encourage honest, heartfelt answers. And what the words don't say, their body language will. Be sensitive. The information you can gather is invaluable.

Be a customer yourself occasionally. Phone your own offices as a customer, disguised of course, and listen to the reception you get. Is it inviting or off-putting? If the latter, polish your employees' phone skills.

And while you're being a customer, ask yourself: What do you like? How do you like to be treated? What makes a shopping or service experience pleasant for you? Pleasant experiences result in repeat business—the best kind.

Listen to your friends. If they tell you the display in the window doesn't work, lose the display. Loyal customers are like friends, too. They care about you and your business. If they tell you something's not working, seriously consider a change. Don't get defensive, even when it's a hard blow being delivered. They're not out to hurt you. They want to help.

Your employees are also excellent gauges of how the business is doing. They deal with customers and their complaints all day long. Do your employees have the tools they need to provide the total experience you are trying to provide? And, by the way, are you taking care of your employees? If you don't treat them well, they are unlikely to treat your customers well. Your employees advertise your quality.

Listen to your employees, too. Encourage them to be open with you. Think of them as an early-warning radar system. They provide an advance warning of business problems. The sooner you deal with something that is out of whack, the better all around. Your employees are in the trenches. When Mrs. Jones stormed out in a huff because of blah, blah, blah, an employee was there. What better place to pick up on issues and start resolving them?

Make quality improvement part of your everyday business culture. Get all employees involved and reward them for their efforts. Encourage them to pay attention to detail. Little things can make a big difference to customers and the image of your business. Of course, hiring the right people in the first place is your best bet.

Your business naturally reflects you. If you're a grouch, everything about your business will be grouchy, including your employees. There's no replacement for self-awareness. Nobody can tell you the hard reality as well as you can. Be your own best critic.

When you wake at two or three or four o'clock in the morning because your internal self wants to talk, listen carefully because truth is being spoken. Be open to it. We instinctively know when we're off track. When our guard is down, as it is in the middle of the night, we let ourselves know. Pay attention to your instincts. Let them be your guide to true quality—and to your success.

**Most successful people
are their own worst critics.**

Conclusion

The baker's dozen commandments in the previous chapters cover the key variables in running a successful small business. People take on the challenges of going on their own for a multitude of reasons. Often they take the plunge because they have no other choice. Better to find out before you start whether you have a fair chance of surviving that choice.

Do you have the right stuff? Are you right for your own business and is your own business right for you? A review of the thirteen commandments might provide the answers.

I. Thou shalt be well organized

If you are a slob at home, you will be a slob in the office. Whether it's keeping your state charter alive or remembering employee anniversaries, smooth running in business depends on organization. If you tend not to pay much attention to details, buy yourself a book or take a course on organizational skills. If you have an eye for detail and love to straighten piles of paper, you possess an important trait for a business owner. But don't drive people around you to distraction by overdoing it. With proper guidance from a professional, your outside organizational requirements will be behind you. Do the same internally by buying the right fixtures and office equipment, and you will spend more time growing your business than you do looking for things.

II. Thou shalt plan thy work and work thy plan

Successful leaders live in the world of tomorrow. Successful people may have difficulty sitting still because they have already experienced the present (when they planned it) and are antsy to move on. The present can, in fact, be anticlimactic. Having anticipated how things will be takes most of the surprise away. But eliminating surprise is a requirement for business survival. You face as many bad surprises as good ones and you must eliminate anything that might catch you unprepared. To successfully manage your business, you must learn to live in the future. If you already do, you're a step ahead of the game. You must plan all the time, constantly quizzing yourself about the consequences of everything you do. Most importantly, you need a clear picture of how you will react to different circumstances. Always have a Plan B.

III. Thou shalt conserve cash

Running out of money is horrible. Yet a business has no guaranteed payday. Once we are up and running and have accumulated some receivables, we can at least anticipate when they will be collected. But unlike when we have a steady job, there is no assurance that next month we will bring in as much as we did this month. Living with this kind of insecurity takes a special attitude. You need to understand the difference between fear and apprehension. Fear is an emotional reaction to the unknown. Apprehension is an intellectual reaction to anticipated variables. When managing cash, it's smart to be apprehensive. It's dangerous to be afraid. Your ability to watch and direct cash every day of your life is critical to managing cash in a tight situation. It's like exercise: You may not want to do it, but you must discipline yourself to do it.

IV. Thou shalt sell effectively

This is where you will most likely thrive. You believe in your product and you believe in yourself. Few things are more fun than going out, meeting folks and making a buck. You will always be your business's best salesperson. Everyone likes to deal with the owner. Take advantage of your special status and sell your heart out. You will be under a gross disadvantage if you do not like to sell. You won't necessarily fail, but your business will miss a huge element that contributes to success. A business owner who does not enjoy promoting the business can overcome it by hiring the right salespeople. When preparing your business plan, remember to factor in this expense.

V. Thou shalt negotiate well

This can be a tough one. If you don't like to negotiate, the consequences are that you will find yourself accepting whatever prices or deals others offer to you. That's not the worst thing in the world, but it does mean that you have less control over certain business issues. As your business grows and things get more complex, the ability to make deals becomes more important. Sooner or later, you will have to get good at it. To negotiate well, above all else have patience. A little sense of humor never hurt either. Care about the other guy's position. To get someone to do something your way, incorporate some of his ways. When the time comes that you are rich and famous, you may demand things. Right now, you are the little guy and every edge the world gives you will be because you persevered in a negotiation.

VI. Thou shalt serve thy employees

Good parents make good employers. The world is full of parenting theories, but all the ones I've heard have some things in common: They all talk about leading the way, about providing tools for success, and about being sincerely interested in the future of the individual. Whatever your personal theory, if it worked with your kids, it will work with your employees.

VII. Thou shalt obey the law

Find yourself a lawyer you like and ask questions. The dumber you think the question is, the more you should make sure you ask it. The really dumb questions are the ones you don't ask. Acquire a working knowledge of the laws that surround you and you will never have to fear them.

VIII. Thou shalt keep excellent records

You need professional help here, too. Find an accountant who will spend some time helping you select and set up an accounting system. Although a manual system may be all you need to get by, join the 21st century and use a computerized one. Whatever you select, pick one you will use and understand. Even if you won't be operating it, you should know how if you have to. Pay someone to handle payroll for you. Payroll services are very reasonable and will save you a bundle of aggravation.

IX. Thou shalt be tax wise

Find a good accountant … period. One other thing: I often wonder if people who constantly grouse about taxes spent the same energy coming up with new ideas about how to make money, which quest would end more successfully?

X. Thou shalt be high tech

This one is most fun. Sometimes when the lights are out, I walk through my office and marvel at the number of little red, yellow and blue lights on all of the high tech gear we've got. It's the sign that we have a going concern. Unless you're made of money, recognize that you can get just as turned on by lights on inexpensive computer equipment as you can on expensive stuff. And there's so much inexpensive stuff to buy. So make sure you have a good time doing it. And remember that a consultant will make this process a lot easier.

XI. Thou shalt be properly insured

To be successful here you need a telephone and some friends or acquaintances who are in business. Find out who they use as an insurance broker and whether they're satisfied. Make the phone call, ask questions, take out your checkbook and you're done.

XII. Thou shalt balance thy life

No matter how hard you try, turn your back on this issue for a moment and it goes out of whack. When you are being consumed by your own business, it's hard to remember why you did this thing in the first place. A normal job begins to look so appealing. It was much easier to schedule your time (it was not) when you had a normal job (if you had a normal job, you never would have left it). You did this thing in the first place to improve your life. Carrying a cell phone on Sundays in case someone needs you is not improving your life. Not taking a three-day weekend occasionally is not improving your life. It sounds easier than it is, but watch yourself carefully. A small business is like quicksand. Stay in touch continually with its hazards.

XIII. Thou shalt deliver fine quality

Delivering a quality product is such common sense. The issue is not whether we *intend* to deliver quality, but whether we *are* delivering quality. In the frenzy of building a business and making more sales, we can easily forget about quality. How quickly are customers being served? How long does it take to fill an order? How good is that stuff we now buy in much larger quantities?

———

We've reached the end of our journey together. Now you are on your own and you are aware of everything you need to be successful. The next step is up to you. No one ever said starting a business would be easy. But it isn't impossible either. The key is in making smart decisions day by day. American author Robert Collier once said that 'Success is the sum of smart efforts, repeated day in and day out.'"

If you're smart you're somewhat uncertain. Although hundreds of thousands of businesses fail each year, hundreds of thousands of businesses succeed. The most important things for you to learn are to leave your ego at the door, be your own worst critic and always, always, always maintain your sense of humor.

ABOUT THE AUTHOR

Dick Sacks grew up in New York City and moved to St. Louis, Missouri, when he was 28. He is a product of both environments and has a broad perspective on businesses and the people who run them.

A graduate of The Baruch School (now Baruch College) of the City University of New York, Dick followed the private accounting track and worked for four New York Stock Exchange listed companies before starting his own consulting firm in 1985.

The Sacks Group, Inc. works exclusively with emerging companies, providing them with both accounting services and financial guidance. His client companies, both present and past, attribute much of their stability to Dick and his staff.

The *Twelve Commandments for Small Business* is the culmination of years of observation of and participation in the day-to-day activities of small companies.

Dick and his wife Bev divide their time between their home in Lake St. Louis, Missouri, and their farm in Santa Fe, Missouri. They have a son, Jeff (and his wife, Teala), a daughter, Allyson, and three grandchildren.